CONTENTS

Part I: Awareness and Exploration

Part II: Developing a Game Plan

Part III: Marketing Yourself

PART I: AWARENESS AND EXPLORATION

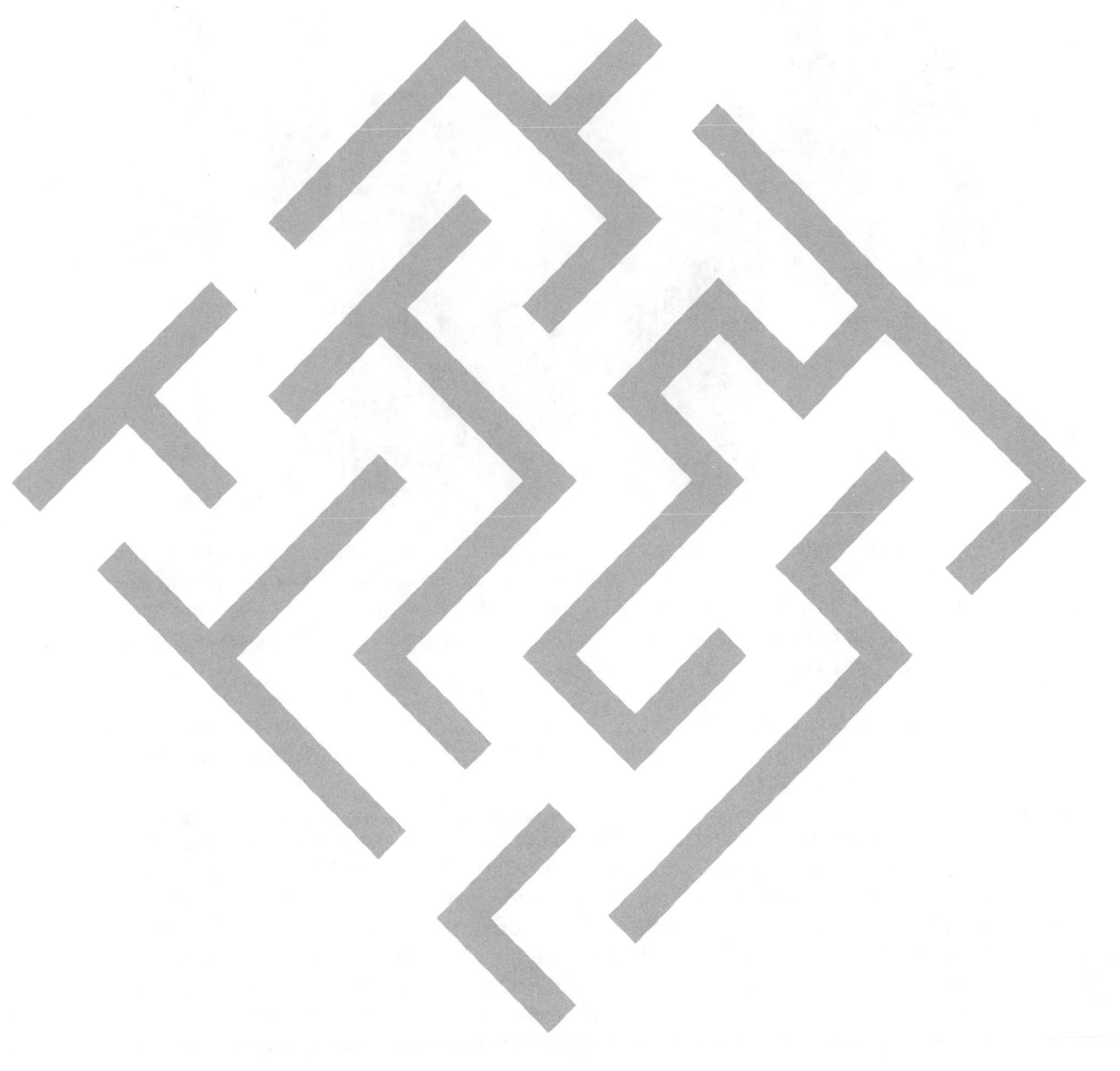

Introduction: Welcome to the Parcours

The ladder has long been used as a metaphor to symbolize the progress of a career. People were supposed to climb the career ladder in one direction. The metaphor of the ladder has been replaced in the 1980s by the Scandinavian *parcours;* a *parcours* is an exercise trail with a set of planned stops where one exercises and develops different muscles or facets of the self.

A career plan is like a *parcours* in that people can have several different occupations or stops as they travel along life's path. Different careers develop or actualize different skills, needs, and values.

Self-assessment, goal determination, and decision-making need to be done at different junctures while traveling the *parcours* of life. People need to decide on goals and a direction as they begin their travel on the *parcours* during the first phase of adulthood, and perhaps several more times during their lives. The exercises in this book are designed to help a young person decide what her or his first adult lifestyle should be like, and to be aware that life and career planning does not end with one's first choice. All adults reach points when life's directions need to be rethought and possibly recharted. They need to push on to new and more challenging stops in the *parcours*.

Life changes, like increasing or decreasing child care responsibilities, mounting financial responsibilities, or simply maturing interests often propel people to find work different from what they originally thought they would do. Many people want to retool for a second career. They may want new training to update and extend educations they obtained when they were younger. *Life Plan* has proved to be a useful tool to thousands of women who were re-entering the job market and seeking a second career.

The image of the career as a series of stops on the *parcours* is applicable to other situations also. People who have worked in declining industries are forced to reassess themselves and chart new courses. Discouragement or boredom are other reasons people look for changes. The open-ended exercises in *Life Plan* are just as meaningful for a person with years of experience in the workforce as for the person with little experience.

By choosing to work through *Life Plan* you have made an important decision about your future. *Life Plan* presents a unique opportunity to engage in a systematic search for the right career. You are beginning a process that will enable you to *plan* your future rather than settle for the first thing that comes along.

USING LIFE PLAN

Part I: Awareness and Exploration

The exercises in this book are appropriate for anyone exploring career options. The process is useful for all: exploration of the self; exploration of the working world; acquisition of the right education; marketing the self to gain the right job.

Life Plan begins with an exploration of your skills, needs, and values. The best career decisions begin with the self—who you are, your strengths, your weaknesses. Only when you have a good self-understanding can you begin to relate to the career options available.

Many people do not really recognize what talents they would be happiest using in their work. Few can readily identify which of their needs must be met if they are to enjoy their work lives. Since work takes up a great deal of time—usually 2000 hours a year for 40-50 years—the motivation to find something you would like doing should be strong.

As a workbook, *Life Plan* is only half written. The part that is not written is about you. The charts, activities, and projects provide an easy-to-follow system to help you discover and assemble an understanding of yourself that can be applied to the jobs available. This can lead to recognition of the kind of work that will bring you personal happiness and fulfillment. There is no such thing as a "good career field." A career field is only good if it is good for the person in question—if it has a growing future and will utilize the person's talents.

Life Plan can be used individually or in group sessions. Professional counselors can analyze objective data, but they can give no helpful guidance without understanding your interests, aptitudes, and values. By using *Life Plan's* procedure of self-understanding, research, and advice interviews, you can become your own excellent career counselor.

The Career Finder starting on page 00 lists several hundred job titles, some of which you probably have never heard. It charts specific job characteristics associated with these occupations to help you relate your self-understanding to the working world. The Career Finder is an exploratory tool which will help you relate your personal interests, preferences, and qualifications for the jobs available.

The Career Finder is a microcosm: it charts many of the characteristics of the job world in miniature. If you find that there are many communications jobs in the Career Finder, that is because there are many communications jobs in the marketplace. If there are relatively few jobs demanding creativity or artistic talent, the numbers reflect the relatively small number of such jobs available.

The Career Finder can help point you in the direction of the right career for you. Formal vocational testing, available in schools and career counseling services, can supplement and refine the direction your career plan should take.

Part II: Developing a Game Plan

Once you have formulated a career objective, you must develop a plan of action. Many people will require more schooling if they are ever going to achieve their desired career. Many promising careers can be begun through training at community colleges or vocational schools, as well as four-year colleges or universities. *Life Plan* can help you select a career with educational qualifications you can achieve, whether through short-term vocational training or long-term college work.

Part III: Marketing Yourself

Marketing yourself is the final phase in developing a career plan. Steps in marketing include developing an effective resume or application form, scouting the available jobs, and interviewing effectively. It is on the basis of how well you sell yourself during your search that you will actually land a promising job. The final chapters in *Life Plan* deal with these elements of selling yourself to an employer.

1. Your Dream Job

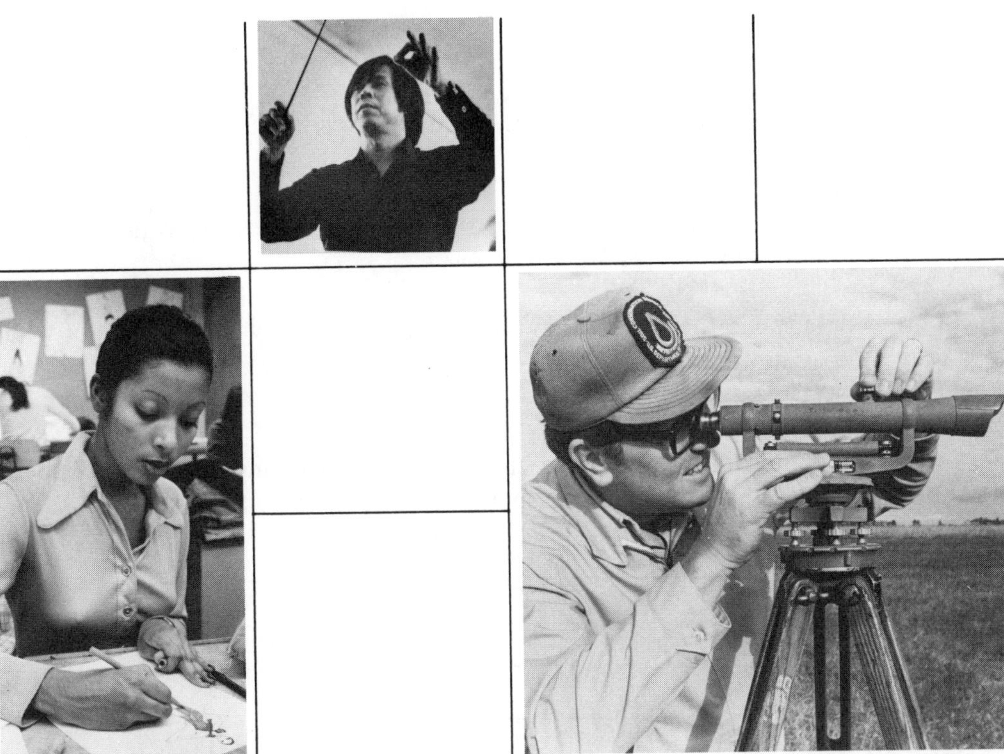

The best clue to the career that will bring you happiness may be as close as your imagination. Try to imagine that you could be anything you want to be, disregarding the money needed to do it, the necessary qualifications and talents. If you could have any job that you wanted in the whole world, what would that job be?

As children grow up they have many ideas about what they want to be. But as people grow older they often become more vague about their possibilities and eventually drift into an occupation more by chance than by choice. When they reach the middle of their lives they often regret not following the fantasies of their youth.

So begin the process of creating your new *Life Plan* by closing your eyes and imagining your dream job. Picture yourself at work in as great a detail as possible. What are you doing? Where do you work? How much do you earn? Spend several minutes conjuring up your fantasy job and when you are finished record the details on the lines below. Write a description, and/or draw a picture on a separate sheet of paper if you see yourself in your job in a certain way. Next, ask yourself how you could make part or all of this dream job come true.

____

____

____

EXPLORING YOUR "SHOULDS"

Too many people do not follow their dreams. Their occupational choices are often influenced by what other people think they should do—the tyranny of the "shoulds."

"You *should* go to college."
"You *should* marry a good housekeeper, good provider, etc."
"You *should* serve your country."
"You *should* earn a lot of money."
"You *should* be a lawyer (or a doctor, a teacher, etc.) because your parent or your grandparent was."

Many people spend their lives doing what *others* think they *should* do, not what *they want* to do. They are tyrannized by the "shoulds" of their parents, role models, friends, and social class.

Evaluate the importance of the expectations of the following people on your career choice. On the scale of one to ten, mark an X to indicate the degree of importance each one's opinions hold.

INFLUENCE	1	2	3	4	5	6	7	8	9	10
Father										
Mother										
Mate										
Brother										
Sister										
Children										
Boyfriend/girlfriend										
Close friends										
Religious leader										
Teacher										
Counselor										
Others										

Think about the strongest "shoulds" that have been imposed on you. Which are the "shoulds" that really matter to you? List them below.

I *should* ______________________________

I *should* ______________________________

I *should* ____

I *should* ____

These feelings, beliefs, and/or values will have some weight in your career choices, but they should be balanced and considered along with others that you hold.

WHO "SHOULD" HOLD WHAT JOB

Being male or female has long imposed many "shoulds" that may not be realistic at all. "Men should hold the positions of power"—jobs that demand physical strength or management of money and people. "Women should perform nurturing work"—an extension of their mothering role. Titles like teacher, nurse, or beautician have traditionally been considered "woman's work."

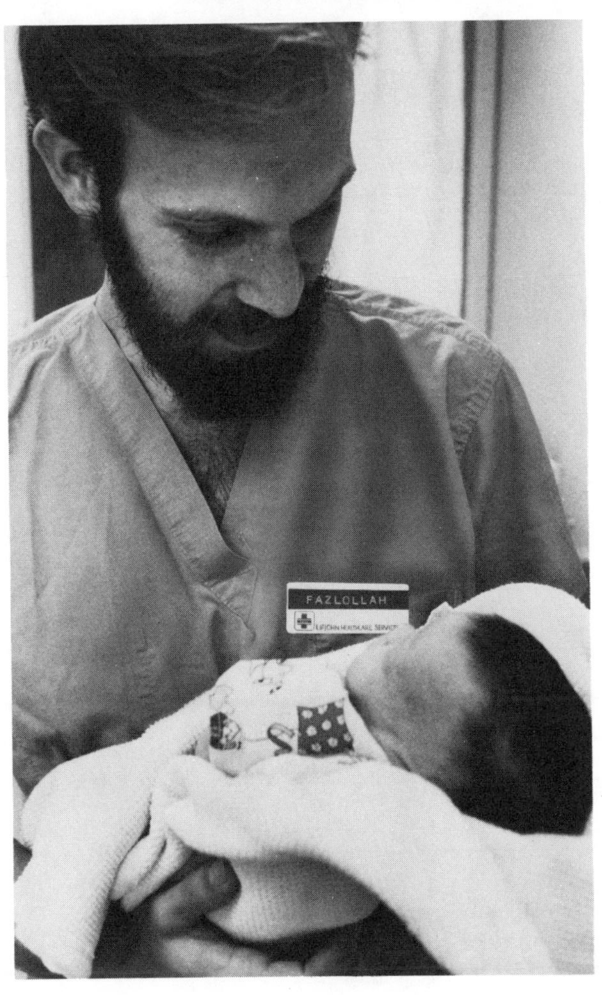

Today, all careers are legally open to both men and women. Yet many people still feel uncomfortable at the thought of performing certain jobs because of their sex. A woman might feel that engineering or construction jobs are closed to her. A man might feel that he could not get hired as a nurse, a secretary, a primary school teacher, or a beautician.

If you are male, try to think of a traditionally "female" job you might like to hold. If you are female, try to think of a traditionally "male" job you would find attractive. Explain why you think you would like the job.

____

____

____

____

BEFORE I DIE I WANT TO...

Career planning concerns your life's mission, what you see the meaning of your life to be. Finish this statement in as many ways as you can.

Before I die I want to...

____

____

____

____

____

____

____

____

Naturally, many of the things you want to do in your lifetime have nothing to do with the world of work. But some of them probably could be part of a job.

Think over the items on your list. Now go back and draw a circle around any of your dreams which could be accomplished by a satisfying paid career.

2. Your Favorite People

Another way to discover clues to your choice of work is to think of the relationships you will form in the job. If you like the people you work with, you might also like the work you are doing. People are attracted to people who have interests and skills similar to their own. The following exercises help define the kinds of people you like best, and relate your preferences to the working world. You can begin to understand the type of person you would like to work with by thinking of specific people you have known. Try to state your reasons for liking and disliking them.

I like people who. . .

____

____

I do not like people who. . .

____

____

Describe the kinds of people you would like to work with:

____

____

YOUR GROUP AT THE PARTY

Suppose you were at a party where everyone was grouped according to thei r interests. You would only have enough time to mingle in two of the groups pictured on this page and the next. Which would you pick first? Which second?

1. *The Body Workers:*
These people enjoy work with their hands or heavy work requiring strength and endurance. They may need special clothing for their work and may be dirty and physically exhausted at the end of their day. Body workers often work with objects, machines, plants, or animals, and they like to be outdoors.

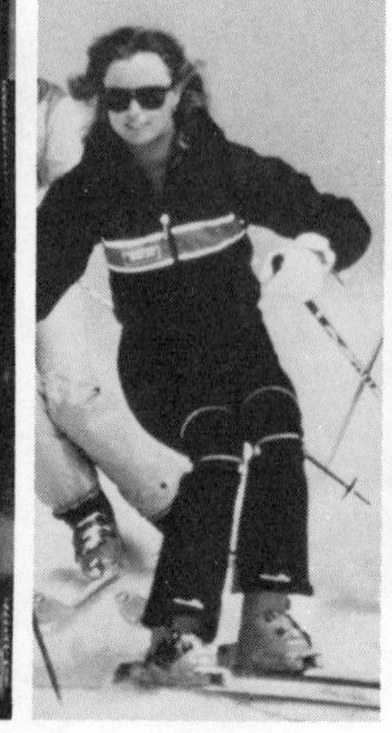

2. *The Data Detail:*
These people use numbers or words in their work in a very exact way. They know that being attentive to detail is important, and they like to work without error. They often have good clerical or math abilities.

3. *The Persuaders:*
Persuaders like to work with people and enjoy convincing others to see things their way. Persuaders often work in sales, law, or politics, where their success is measured by how well they influence others.

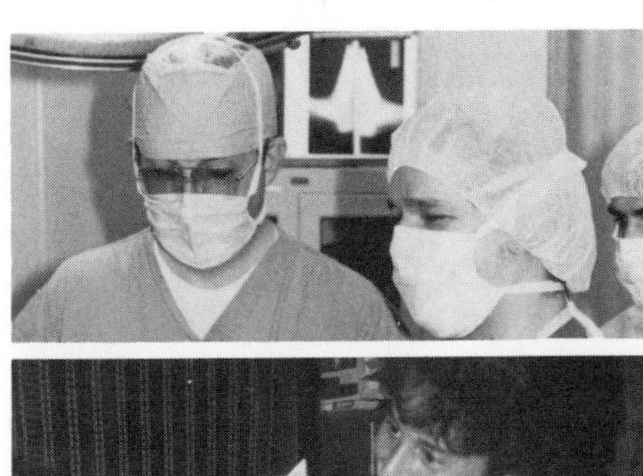
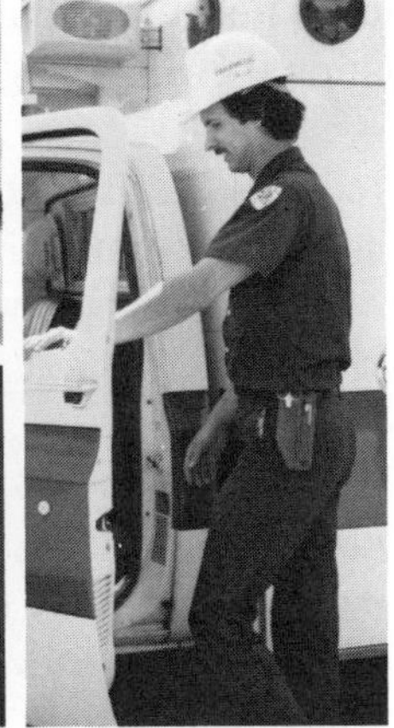

4. *The Service Workers:*
Service workers find their reward in helping people: teaching, nursing, counseling. They often work in schools, hospital, or social agencies.

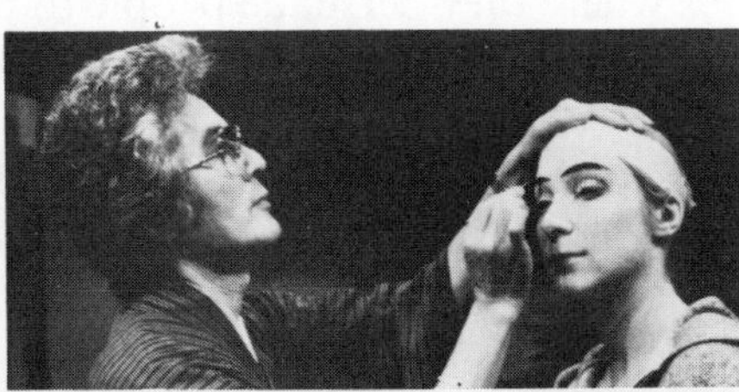

5. *The Creative Artists:*
Creative artists are artistic people who express themselves through music, dance, drama, writing, or art. Many creative artists can only afford to work at their jobs part-time because demand (and pay) for many creative workers' jobs is low.

6. *The Investigators:*
Investigators enjoy asking the questions *Why?* and *How?* in their work. They work with scientific or technical information, applying it to new situations.

Which group would you instinctively be drawn to and enjoy being with the longest time? ______________________________

After half an hour, if you had to move, what group would you choose second? ______________________________

Every job in the world fits into one of, or a combination of, the catego ries described in the ''picnic'' exercise above. Each group attracts a differen t kind of coworker and involves a different kind of work. The Career Finder on pag es 00-00 codes each occupation into one of these occupational groups:

I.	Body Workers	Frequently called blue collar workers, these people usually work with tools or machines in skilled trades, technical or service jobs. Body workers are typically practical, rugged, and aggressive.
II.	Data Detail	Part of the ''white collar workers,'' these people hold office jobs involving clerical or numerical tasks. These workers are usually good at following instructions and attending to detail work.
III.	Persuaders	Usually holding management or sales positions, these workers hold jobs where they persuade people to perform some kind of action.
IV.	Service Workers	Often working in education, health care, or social welfare, these workers hold jobs where they teach, heal, or help people.
V.	Creative Artists	These people's work involves using words, music, or art in a creative way.
VI.	Investigators	Usually performing scientific or laboratory work, investigators research how the world is put together and how to solve problems.

To what group would a person performing your Dream Job (described on page five) belong? For example, if your Dream Job is to be a movie star, a person with that job would probably be found in group V, the Creative Artists. My fantasy job belongs to group ____, or a combination of groups ____ and ____.

Is the group to which your fantasy job belongs the same as one of the groups you selected in the party exercise? If so, this is a strong indication that your greatest work satisfaction may be found in a career in that category.

3. Your Needs

Psychologist Abraham Maslow studied the relationship between needs and motivation for many years, and suggested that it is what we need that motivates the ways that we act.

He developed a hierarchy of needs which he diagrammed as a pyramid, showing five levels of needs which motivate us.

At the most basic level, Level 1, is *Survival.* At this level, we strive for food, clothing, and shelter—our basic needs to stay alive.

At Level 2 is *Safety.* At this level, people strive for more security—savings, insurance, safe working places, and safe homes and communities.

Level 3 is *Belongingness.* To achieve belongingness, people work for good relationships with their families and friends, recreational opportunities, and associations with groups in their communities.

Level 4 is *Esteem.* At this level, a person may strive for recognition and respect, in their life's work, and in the community at large. At work, they may seek more autonomy, the right to schedule their own time, and take more responsibility.

Level 5 is *Self-Actualization.* Level 5 is the highest level, at which the individual strives for the highest development of personal potential, including the establishment of individual goals, and the ongoing growth of personal freedom, creativity, responsibility, mastery of skills and accomplishment that is valued by the community, family and friends.

Many people work to achieve the basic needs of levels one and two. These needs must be fulfilled before the higher level needs concern a person greatly. If a person has enough income, basic needs can be met. A person's work enables her or him to be with other people and to maintain a family, thus fulfilling the level three need for belonging.

As a person begins to fulfill needs in level four, work takes on more importance. It becomes important to develop a sense of confidence, master achievement in one's life. For many people, their sense of self-esteem comes from their work.

Once the first four levels of needs have been largely fulfilled, a person craves self-actualization. This deals with the concept of having a mission in life. This need causes some independently wealthy people to continue to work. Work brings more than just money as a reward.

Consider your own feelings about these needs, and record some of your thoughts in notes on the lines below.

What level need do you think motivates you the most?____________________

____

____

____

____

____

____

What could you do to fulfill your need for

belongingness?________________________________

esteem?____________________________________

self-actualization?______________________________

Choose two or three people in your community, or in positions of leadership, about whom you have some substantial information. Perhaps a successful teacher, religious leader, business person, family member, or neighbor, whom you know. Think over the levels on which these persons have developed their lives. Remember that to be self-actualizing, the person does not have to be rich or famous; the person may be recognized and valued within a particular community or family.

When you have chosen two or or three possibilities, write in their names below, and think over how they have fulfilled their needs at Levels 1, 2, 3, 4 and 5. Consider how some of their choices and methods would work out for you. Would you choose some of the same actions? Which ones would be of value to you, as you plan your own career and lifestyle?

Person #1:____

____

____

____

____

Person #2:____

____

____

____

____

Person #3:____

____

____

____

____

4. The Interest Indicator

Defining what you like to do can help you find a potentially satisfying career. If you do what you like to do and you enjoy your work, you will do it better. Knowing what gives you pleasure is a key clue in finding the right occupational "fit."

The Interest Indicator Sheet on the next page will give you a chance to rate some of your activities.

Your life has been different from anyone else's life already. You may not have thought of it that way before. But those different experiences have allowed you to learn things that no one else has learned in exactly the same way. Of course, some of the experiences are similar to those of other people. And some of the things you have learned from them are similar to the things your friends have learned. But the total combination that you have lived through so far is yours and yours alone. You have lived through things that you liked, and things that you didn't like.

Try to think of the experiences that you have really enjoyed. Was it getting a new puppy? Was it helping your grandmother in her garden? Was it helping paint apartments last summer with your uncle? Whatever you can think of that really made you feel good is something worth considering. And the things that you enjoy that are special to you may provide you with the best clues to what kind of work you will be good at, and enjoy the most.

INTEREST INDICATOR SHEET

In the column below, list 10 things you have enjoyed doing in the past four years. Include special school projects, extracurricular activities, hobbies, and/or summer and after-school activities. Read the statements to the right and put a check in the square next to each activity on your list about which the statement is true.

Try to think of activities that you have done that other people have not done.

	This activity involves some kind of risk—financial, physical, or emotional.	This activity gives you a joyful feeling.	You believe this activity will help you grow as a person.	You spend more than $3 each time you do this activity.	You would like to let others know that you do this.	You spent at least four hours each week doing this activity in the last month.	You spend time reading, thinking or worrying about this activity.	You consciously choose this over other possible activities.
1.								
2.								
3.								
4.								
5.								
6.								
7.								
8.								
9.								
10.								

INTEREST/SKILL INTERSECTIONS

The more markings you have next to an item, the more likely that this activity is one of your top pleasure-producing interests. Select the top five activities from your Interest Indicator Sheet according to the number of marks next to each item—the activity with the most marks being first. List these top five interests in the column to the left, below.

In the column to the right, list challenges that are related to each interest. What must you know how to do in order to complete that kind of task well? What skills will you want to develop further?

INTERESTS	CHALLENGES
(sample) design original needle point pieces	Work requiring self-expression
1.	
2.	
3.	
4.	
5.	

WHAT KIND OF WORK DO YOU LIKE BEST?

The following lists describe activities performed in many different occupations. They will help you define the kinds of work you like doing. Decide how interested you are in performing the jobs listed. Read each and try to determine your interest in it. Don't consider salary, status, or necessary education.

For each item decide your degree of interest in the activity and circle the number describing your interest. Do this on each of the six pages which follow.

0 1 2 3	Not interested. Would detest doing this work.
0 1 2 3	Slight interest. Would do it if you had to.
0 1 2 3	Interested. You would enjoy doing this work.
0 1 2 3	Extremely interested. You would love a job where you could perform this activity.

INTEREST INDICATOR
GROUP 1

The Body Workers

		Not interested	Slight interest	Interested	Extremely interested
1.	Tune pianos	0	1	2	3
2.	Cut and style hair	0	1	2	3
3.	Reupholster furniture	0	1	2	3
4.	Test and analyze automobile engines	0	1	2	3
5.	Farm land and tend farm animals	0	1	2	3
6.	Run a projector in a movie theater	0	1	2	3
7.	Prepare food in a restaurant	0	1	2	3
8.	Install electrical wiring	0	1	2	3
9.	Repair home defects	0	1	2	3
10.	Set type for books or newspapers	0	1	2	3
11.	Care for plants in a nursery	0	1	2	3
12.	Repair shoes	0	1	2	3
13.	Teach carpentry	0	1	2	3
14.	Draft plans for room additions	0	1	2	3
15.	Make dental plates and false teeth	0	1	2	3
16.	Run dry cleaning equipment	0	1	2	3
17.	Park cars at a parking lot	0	1	2	3
18.	Repair watches and jewelry	0	1	2	3
19.	Lay brick for new buildings	0	1	2	3
20.	Make leather products like belts	0	1	2	3
21.	Cut and package meat in a grocery store	0	1	2	3
22.	Repair faulty plumbing	0	1	2	3
23.	Drive a taxicab	0	1	2	3
24.	Make alterations on clothing	0	1	2	3
25.	Pilot an airplane	0	1	2	3
TOTALS					

INTEREST INDICATOR
GROUP II

The Data Detail

		Not interested	Slight interest	Interested	Extremely interested
1.	Connect long distance telephone calls	0	1	2	3
2.	Make travel reservations	0	1	2	3
3.	Review credit applications	0	1	2	3
4.	Estimate cost of repairing damaged autos	0	1	2	3
5.	Collect money from customers and make change	0	1	2	3
6.	Proofread type for publication	0	1	2	3
7.	Shelve books at a library	0	1	2	3
8.	Duplicate printed materials	0	1	2	3
9.	File records and correspondence	0	1	2	3
10.	Run a telegraph machine	0	1	2	3
11.	Serve as a data processing keypunch operator	0	1	2	3
12.	Assist doctors with office work	0	1	2	3
13.	Keep records of business transactions	0	1	2	3
14.	Investigate insurance claims	0	1	2	3
15.	Teach typing and shorthand	0	1	2	3
16.	Count, sort, and store supplies	0	1	2	3
17.	Record court proceedings	0	1	2	3
18.	Take shorthand and type letters	0	1	2	3
19.	Sort mail	0	1	2	3
20.	Estimate costs and buy business materials	0	1	2	3
21.	Prepare financial and tax reports	0	1	2	3
22.	Operate business machines	0	1	2	3
23.	Maintain payroll records	0	1	2	3
24.	Keep detailed records of payments and sales	0	1	2	3
25.	Write business letters	0	1	2	3
TOTALS					

INTEREST INDICATOR
GROUP III

The Persuaders

		Not interested	Slight interest	Interested	Extremely interested
1.	Investigate insurance claims	0	1	2	3
2.	Oversee company's wage and salary plans	0	1	2	3
3.	Sell automobiles to customers	0	1	2	3
4.	Recruit workers for a business	0	1	2	3
5.	Sell merchandise across a counter in a store	0	1	2	3
6.	Manage a post office	0	1	2	3
7.	Demonstrate products like food, appliances	0	1	2	3
8.	Sell insurance to prospective customers	0	1	2	3
9.	Manage a hotel or store	0	1	2	3
10.	Help people transact business in a bank	0	1	2	3
11.	Serve as head of a hospital	0	1	2	3
12.	Appraise real estate value	0	1	2	3
13.	Act as a judge at trials	0	1	2	3
14.	Interview possible employees	0	1	2	3
15.	Announce the news on radio or TV	0	1	2	3
16.	Manage a gas station	0	1	2	3
17.	Buy grains at a commodity exchange	0	1	2	3
18.	Run a floral shop	0	1	2	3
19.	Serve meals and drinks on an airplane	0	1	2	3
20.	Guide travelers on European tours	0	1	2	3
21.	Direct recreation programs at park district	0	1	2	3
22.	Manage an apartment building	0	1	2	3
23.	Judge trials and legal proceedings	0	1	2	3
24.	Argue legal matters before a jury	0	1	2	3
25.	Contract for building materials and labor	0	1	2	3
	TOTALS				

INTEREST INDICATOR
GROUP IV

The Service Workers

		Not interested	Slight interest	Interested	Extremely interested
1.	Manage welfare payments	0	1	2	3
2.	Serve as a nurse in a hospital	0	1	2	3
3.	Coach an athletic team	0	1	2	3
4.	Help people who are poor or in trouble	0	1	2	3
5.	Be an officer in Foreign Service	0	1	2	3
6.	Attend to the spiritual needs of people	0	1	2	3
7.	Teach history in a high school	0	1	2	3
8.	Plan meals and diets for elderly people	0	1	2	3
9.	Seat customers at a restaurant	0	1	2	3
10.	Teach children in a nursery school	0	1	2	3
11.	Direct funerals	0	1	2	3
12.	Help keep law and order in a community	0	1	2	3
13.	Be a politician in a state legislature	0	1	2	3
14.	Manage a home for your own family	0	1	2	3
15.	Serve as a fire fighter in a fire department	0	1	2	3
16.	Play on a professional athletic team	0	1	2	3
17.	Teach sports in a park district	0	1	2	3
18.	Raise children	0	1	2	3
19.	Give manicures	0	1	2	3
20.	Cater elegant dinner parties	0	1	2	3
21.	Check out books at a library	0	1	2	3
22.	Clean teeth and teach dental hygiene	0	1	2	3
23.	Advise people who want to make career choices	0	1	2	3
24.	Care for old people in a retirement home	0	1	2	3
25.	Teach handicapped children	0	1	2	3
TOTALS					

INTEREST INDICATOR
GROUP V

The Creative Artists

	Not interested	Slight interest	Interested	Extremely interested
1. Teach philosophy	0	1	2	3
2. Draw comics or animated films	0	1	2	3
3. Plan public relations for a political candidate	0	1	2	3
4. Perform as a singer or dancer before an audience	0	1	2	3
5. Teach literature in a college	0	1	2	3
6. Write stories or books about people and places	0	1	2	3
7. Conduct an orchestra	0	1	2	3
8. Play in a band or orchestra	0	1	2	3
9. Paint pictures	0	1	2	3
10. Design and draw plans for buildings	0	1	2	3
11. Photograph people and events	0	1	2	3
12. Review movies for a newspaper	0	1	2	3
13. Design interiors for homes or stores	0	1	2	3
14. Direct a community theater	0	1	2	3
15. Paint posters for stores	0	1	2	3
16. Layout a magazine	0	1	2	3
17. Set up displays in store windows	0	1	2	3
18. Teach art in a high school	0	1	2	3
19. Design furniture	0	1	2	3
20. Write radio program scripts	0	1	2	3
21. Edit books	0	1	2	3
22. Teach dancing	0	1	2	3
23. Interpret foreign languages	0	1	2	3
24. Create sculptures	0	1	2	3
25. Design fashions	0	1	2	3
TOTALS				

INTEREST INDICATOR
GROUP VI

The Investigators

		Not interested	Slight interest	Interested	Extremely interested
1.	Study, care for, and protect animals	0	1	2	3
2.	Take X-ray photographs at a hospital	0	1	2	3
3.	Study and search for uses of atomic energy	0	1	2	3
4.	Study the way human beings behave	0	1	2	3
5.	Check and control a county's water supply	0	1	2	3
6.	Design and construct airplanes	0	1	2	3
7.	Study the stars and changes in the heavens	0	1	2	3
8.	Test fertilizers and ways of growing crops	0	1	2	3
9.	Predict the financial conditions of the country	0	1	2	3
10.	Develop chemical products in a laboratory	0	1	2	3
11.	Treat sick animals	0	1	2	3
12.	Search for and study artifacts from past civilizations	0	1	2	3
13.	Study oceanic life	0	1	2	3
14.	Fill teeth cavities	0	1	2	3
15.	Predict the weather for the National Weather Service	0	1	2	3
16.	Fly commercial airplanes	0	1	2	3
17.	Operate a computer	0	1	2	3
18.	Test materials in a laboratory	0	1	2	3
19.	Repair televisions and radios	0	1	2	3
20.	Collect and classify precious stones	0	1	2	3
21.	Diagnose illnesses and prescribe medication	0	1	2	3
22.	Mix and dispense medications at a drugstore	0	1	2	3
23.	Complete medical tests in a lab or clinic	0	1	2	3
24.	Perform surgery in a hospital	0	1	2	3
25.	Teach mathematics in a high school	0	1	2	3
	TOTALS				

Directions for totaling

Now go back and add together the numbers in each section. Each zero circled counts nothing. The ones are worth one point each; the twos are worth two points each; the threes are worth three points each. Write in the total score for each section on the line marked Total.

Compare the total figures in your Interest Indicator (Pages 17-18). What two groups received the highest number? (Group 1: Body Workers; Group II: Data Detail; Group III: Persuaders; Group IV: The Service Workers; Group V: Creative Artists; Group VI: Investigators)

Which two groups did you select in the party exercise on pages 10-11? ____________

The occupations that would interest you most are probably combinations of the groups you chose on the Interest Indicator and those selected in the party exercise.

Every job has characteristics of more than one occupational group; some parts of a job will resemble one occupational group, while other parts will resemble another. Thus in the Career Finder a two letter code has been given to each job title. For example, the Code for Teacher is SP, meaning that the job Teacher most resembles the service workers group occupations and also the persuader group occupations, though somewhat less.

You can devise codes of occupations that might interest you. List some possible codes, combining your party and Interest Indicator choices. (For example, if you chose creative artists and service workers on the party exercise and service workers and persuaders on the Interest Indicator, possible codes are CS, PS, SC, SP, CP.) Write in your own codes here:

____

____

____

Turn to the Career Finder on pages 62-96. Using the two-letter codes in the left column of the Career Finder, find up to five occupations that combine what you like to do and the kinds of people you like to be with. Write them below.

____

____

____

5. Skill Identification

Decide whether the following statements are *myths* or *facts*.

_______________ I have no important skills and talents.

_______________ Everyone is aware of her or his talents and skills.

_______________ Most skills used in jobs are learned in school.

_______________ Skills learned at home or on the street are rarely applicable to a job.

All of the above are common myths about skills. Most people wear blinders when they look at themselves. People come equipped with screening mechanisms that shield them from the validity of their experiences and an appreciation of their own self worth. The fact is that skills learned not only in school but also in personal life are applicable to many jobs. In one survey of top managers, 51 percent rated an ability to get along with people as the most important skill they look for when hiring employees.

This exercise is intended to get rid of the blinders you may be wearing and open your eyes to the skills you have acquired in your life. It will help you to recognize your innermost talents.

In the diagonal blanks at the top of the chart on page 28, fill in ten accomplishments, jobs, or roles you have had. Emphasize parts of your life that you feel good about, regardless of whether they were formally recognized. The examples may be achievements like "I starred in the school play," "I learned to sew a tailored suit," "I tuned up an automobile," or "I taught my little sister to tie her shoes." The examples could be paid jobs—babysitting, lawn care, or waiting on tables in a restaurant. Examples of different roles are student, worker, friend, housekeeper. Try to select examples, large or small, of things you have enjoyed doing and you feel good about. Think of some examples of the *best* you have ever done—the best personal relationship you ever had, the best paper you ever wrote.

Then read the list of skills and mark an X next to each skill you performed while completing your accomplishments. Put an 0 if you enjoyed performing that skill.

The example is filled out to describe the skills used by a girl working at a fast food franchise. She puts together customer's orders, so there is an X before "assemble." She sometimes sets up the milkshake machine and enjoys doing it. Thus there is an 0 before "operates tools." Reading, writing, and remembering are all a part of waiting on customers, so those skills are checked too. She has little opportunity to express herself in the work itself, so no items are marked under "freedom to use own ideas." Communicating with people, managing money, calculating figures, working rapidly with numbers, and collecting money are all a part of waiting on people and being a wage earner, so these skills, too, are marked.

SKILL CHART

List 10 work, volunteer, school or leisure experiences here:

Because I did this . . .

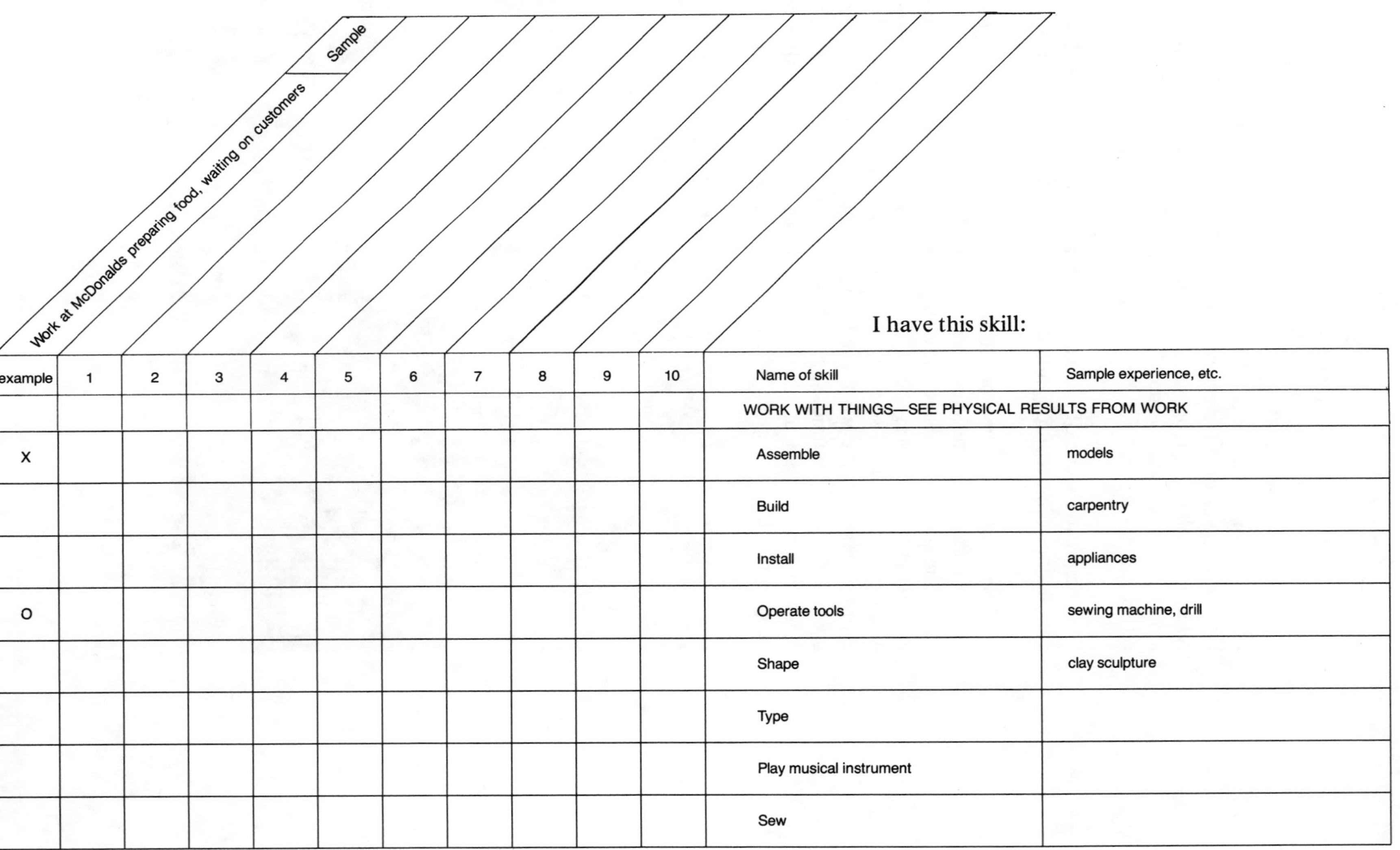

I have this skill:

example	1	2	3	4	5	6	7	8	9	10	Name of skill	Sample experience, etc.
Sample: Work at McDonalds preparing food, waiting on customers												
											WORK WITH THINGS—SEE PHYSICAL RESULTS FROM WORK	
X											Assemble	models
											Build	carpentry
											Install	appliances
O											Operate tools	sewing machine, drill
											Shape	clay sculpture
											Type	
											Play musical instrument	
											Sew	

											Cut	scisssors
											Photograph	snapshots, videotape
											Paint	artwork
											Draw	
X											Wash	cars, clothing
											Feed	babies, elderly
											Press	ironing
											Repair	cars, toys
											Drive	vehicles

WORK WITH IDEAS—USE INTELLECT

X											Read	instructions
X											Write	letters, orders
X											Instruct	
											Edit	rewrite
X											Remember	instructions, names
											Report	
											Translate	foreign language
											Speak	before groups

											Summarize	club minutes
											Describe	writing letters
											Interview	

WORK WITH PEOPLE—ASSIST THEM IN HELPING RELATIONSHIP

											Assist	disabled person
X											Be sensitive to emotions	during disagreement
											Listen/understand	
X											Establish rapport	with new acquaintance
											Encourage	
											Raise other's self concept	
											Heal	physical wounds
											Advise	
											Draw out people	someone who is shy
											Reconcile	bring people together
X											Serve	take care of physical needs

WORK WITH PEOPLE USING PLEASING PERSONALITY

X											Initiate relationship	with stranger at school
											Organize	in a club

											Direct others	officer in a club
											Manage	direct other's work
											Instruct	explanations
											Converse	carry on lively conversations
											Entertain	parties, make people laugh

WORK REQUIRING SELF EXPRESSION—FREEDOM TO USE OWN IDEAS

											Imagine	think of new ways to do things
											Invent, Compose	stories, songs
											Improvise, adapt	use equipment for purpose other than it was intended
											Conceive	think of new ways to do things
											Design	handicrafts
											Create symbols or images	filmmaking, artwork
											Combine colors	interior design, fashion coordination
											Convey emotions and ideas	acting, public speaking, dancing
											Use words imaginatively	creative writing

WORK AS PART OF A TEAM

											Share credit, appreciation	
X											Cooperate	

											Consult	
X											Help	
X											Take instructions	

WORK DEMANDING PHYSICAL STAMINA

											Perform	act on stage
											Carry, lift	
											Deliver	
X											Operate machines	snowblower, lawn mower
											Paint	walls
											Use eye-hand-foot coordination	walking, climbing, running, skiing
											Use muscular coordination	gymnastics, swimming
											Use eye-hand coordination	racquet sports, ball playing
											Care for animals	groom

WORK WITH DETAILS

											Inventory, count	store, kitchen
X											Calculate, compute	bankbook

O											Manage money	tax records
											Budget	allocating expenses
											Remember numbers	phone numbers
O											Work rapidly with numbers	calculate in head
											Estimate	total future charges
X											Collect	cashier
											Measure	cooking
											Use statistics	conduct survey
											Classify	filing
											Remember facts	objective tests
											Follow detailed instructions	assemble bike
											Classify	
											Record	
											File	
											Retrieve	
											Transcribe	shorthand

WORK WITH PEOPLE, MOTIVATING AND PERSUADING THEM

											Organize, recruit, enlist	mobilize people to action
											Raise funds	collect for charity
											Stimulate	give rousing speech
O											Sell, negotiate	garage sale
											Persuade	debate, editorials
											Lead, direct others	cheerleading, team captain
											Supervise	child care
											Motivate	persuade someone to change
											Arbitrate	settle family argument
											Divert	draw people's attention from one thing to another

Recognizing your skills is important in deciding what career you would like to try. Look back over the skill chart and decide which three areas you are strongest in, putting a check before the skill you feel you can legitimately say you possess.

		Career Finder Number
______	Work with things	7
______	Work with ideas	8
______	Work with people—helping them	9
______	Work with people—using pleasing personality	10
______	Work requiring self expression	12
______	Working as part of a team	13
______	Work demanding physical stamina	21
______	Work with details	22
______	Work motivating and persuading people	24

RELATING YOUR SKILLS TO DESIRABLE CAREERS

The nine skill titles used in the preceeding chart are the same as the job characteristics listed in the Career Finder pages 63-96. Use the Career Finder or your imagination and knowledge of the outside world to detect jobs which would use skills you now have. For example, if your strongest job skills are 7, 13, and 22, you might consider being a lithographer.

SKILL/CAREER RELATIONSHIP

List your top three skills and try to think of an attractive career option that uses these skills. Write down the name of the career whether or not you have *all* the skills needed for it now.

Skill	*Attractive career which uses skill*
1.______________________	1.______________________
2.______________________	2.______________________
3.______________________	3.______________________

What skills do you need to develop for each career you find appealing?

Appealing Career	*Skill to develop*
1.________________	1.________________
2.________________	2.________________
3.________________	3.________________

How can the missing skills be acquired?

Missing skills	*Way to acquire missing skills*
1.________________	1.________________
2.________________	2.________________
3.________________	3.________________

Now delve deeper into your memory bank and try to identify other unique experiences which might give you a special background that others have not had. Think of careers experienced by members of your family or friends from which you have learned a great deal; or perhaps you have been part of special projects that other people have not experienced. Think of unusual people you have known, books that have taught you special things. Beside each experience that you list, try to define the skill that you feel you have obtained as a result of that experience.

Experience	*Skills*
(Sample)	
Daughter of writer/publisher	Know what is involved in getting something into print.
Owner and caretaker of four pets	Good understanding of animal care
Avid sports fan	Know rules for many games
Read many mysteries	Know how crimes are solved

Experience	*Skills*
________________	________________
________________	________________
________________	________________

Now use the following Career Investigation Sheet to investigate another career that interests you. List the career, and think it over as you write.

CAREER INVESTIGATION SHEET

Interesting-sounding career: ______________________________

____

	Won't Accept	Unsure	Will Accept
Training or education requirements: ______________________________ ______________________________ ______________________________			
Job description: (what would you do all day?) ______________________________ ______________________________ ______________________________			
Work environment: (office/factory, indoor/outdoor) ______________________________ ______________________________ ______________________________			
Earning potential: (how much will I start earning? how much will I eventually make?) ______________________________ ______________________________ ______________________________			
Employment outlook: (will there be jobs after I complete the necessary education?) ______________________________ ______________________________ ______________________________			

6. Job Characteristics

Think about the following questions:

How much education would you like your career to require?

Where do you want to work?

Do you want to work with people, information, or things?

How much freedom of self-expression do you require?

Do you want to work alone or as part of a team?

Do you want to supervise others, or do you want them to supervise you?

How much responsibility do you want?

How do you feel about working with details?

How do you feel about performing the same task over and over?

Knowing the answers to some of these questions can help you find a satisfying career. Begin the process by deciding the importance of the following job factors:

JOB ENVIRONMENT
Pleasant surroundings
Private working space
Piped-in music
Exercise facilities
Company cafeteria
Windows or view
Nonsmoking environment
Work primarily outdoors
Travel frequently

COMPENSATION
Fair salary
Commission on sales
Royalty
Bonuses
Frequent salary review
Health insurance
Dental insurance
Company car
Tuition reimbursements
Predictable promotions
Chance to advance rapidly

TIME
Set work schedule
Flexible work schedule
Extensive vacations
Overtime
No overtime
Work to take home
Work weekends
Night work
Regular lunch hours
Regular routine
Paid holidays
Summers free

PEOPLE CONTACT
Work alone
Supervise others
Work independently
Work closely supervised
Work in large organization
Work in small business

SCHOOLING REQUIRED
High school
Apprenticeship
Technical school
Associates' degree
Bachelor's degree
Master's degree
Doctorate

Now look back over your list of wants and compose an advertisement you could write describing the characteristics of the job you want: ______

Think over the characteristics you have listed on the previous page and consider what jobs have many or even all of these characteristics. List the jobs below, and also jot down any thoughts you have about the limitations the jobs might pose. Would you need to know more about requirements? Would you need additional training? Would you need to move to a different part of the country? Write down your thoughts, after each job name, and keep your list for further refer ence as you consider your career possibilities.

Job: ______________________________

____

____

____

____

____

____

Job: ______________________________

____

____

____

____

____

____

Job: ______________________________

____

____

____

____

____

____

7. Rewards and Satisfactions

Work differs in what you do all day: the work itself, the people you work with, and the kinds of rewards you receive. The rewards are not just money, but the kind of feeling you get from doing the job.

What is rewarding to one person may be unimportant to another. Some people want to be rich. Some want to help others. Some want to create beautiful art. The secret is to define the rewards that are important to you, because you will never be motivated until you find an activity that is meaningful to you.

Everyone needs the feeling that what they are doing is worthwhile. The more people understand the value of their work, the more motivated they will be to do it.

REWARDS AND SATISFACTIONS

On the next three pages are pictures of six different kinds of workers. Write a caption for each of these pictures. Explain why you think each person could enjoy what he or she is doing—what the rewards of the work are.

Caption:

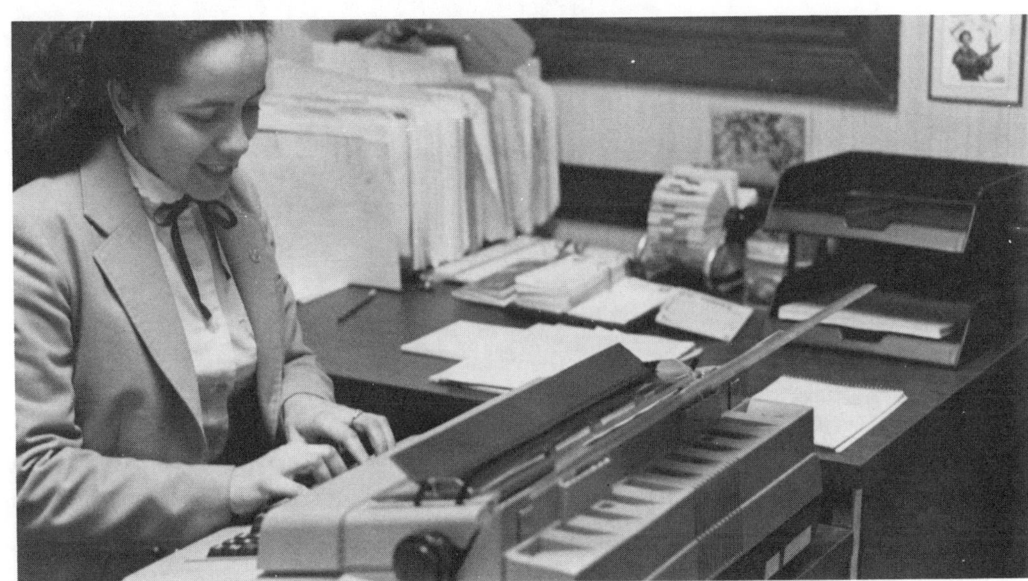

Caption:

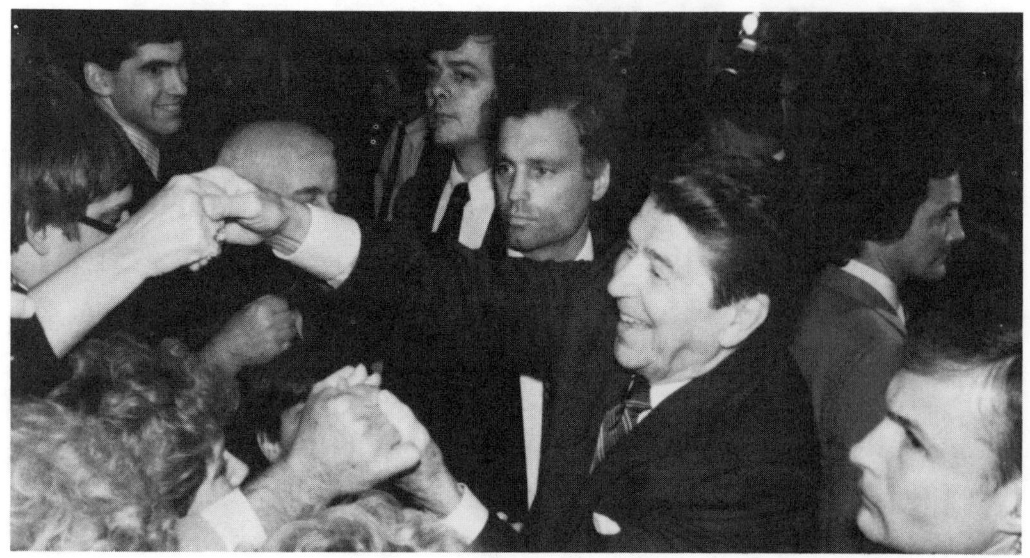

Caption:____

____

____

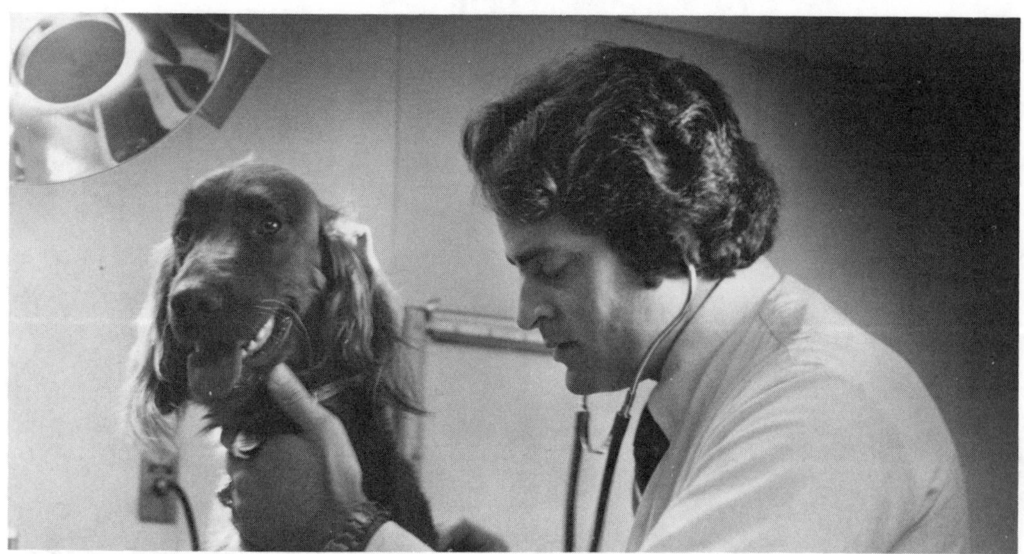

Caption:____

____

____

Caption:____

____

____

Caption:____

____

____

Different people find rewards and motivation from different things. For some, satisfaction comes from a sense of achievement at seeing the work that is completed. These people are often called the **Body Workers.** They enjoy seeing the real, concrete results of their work.

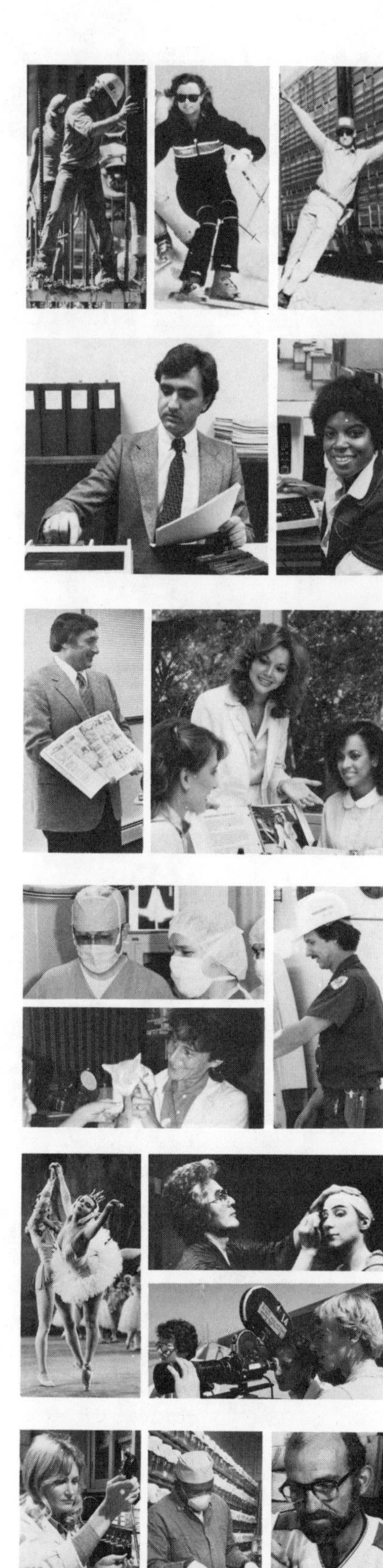

Others feel good at helping an organization run smoothly, being part of an efficient business. The people who are motivated by this kind of reward are often the **Data Detail** people.

The **Persuaders** enjoy seeing things happen. They have a sense of achievement from mobilizing people and ideas. Many persuaders are paid in proportion to their achievements, so money is often a payoff for being a successful persuader.

For the **Service Workers** the joy of helping people is usually the greatest reward.

The thrill of the creative process, of being involved in the conception and actualization of an idea is the greatest reward of the **Creative Artists.**

The **Investigators** enjoy analyzing things—seeing how they work.

The following list includes some of the many different rewards of working. Select the five rewards that you would like most to be part of your career, putting a check before the reason.

__________ Have responsibilities which change frequently

__________ Work in situations with little room for error

__________ Have close working relationships with others

__________ Do projects alone, without much contact

__________ Pit abilities against others with clear win-lose results

__________ Work under pressure

__________ Control the work or destiny of others

__________ Search for knowledge or truth

__________ Create new programs without following a previous format

__________ Study and appreciate beauty

__________ Have a predictable work routine

__________ Work without much direction from others

__________ Work on own time schedule

__________ Other rewards____

Now try to think of three careers which would provide all or most of the rewards you desire.

____

____

____

Use career references, the Career Finder in this book, the want ad lists in the newspaper, or any other sources to give you ideas of possibilities. Consider the rewards and satisfactions of each possibility carefully.

8. Getting Field Experience

Most career fields have volunteer or part-time opportunities available where a young person can gain experience that will help in making an informed career choice. All that is needed is a willingness to give your time on a regular, scheduled basis.

"I majored in special education in college, did my student teaching in my senior year, and discovered that it wasn't for me. I sure wasted a lot of time and money, majoring in something I don't want to do."

—Sue, a 22-year old woman, now cleans airplanes for an airline.

"I'm a trainee in a computer programming department but I don't enjoy working in an office. I can't stand being cooped up all the time. It's a good job, but not for me. Trouble is, I can't afford to give up the salary while I check out things I'd like to do better."

—Dan, a 27-year old man, working in a corporate programming department.

If Sue had volunteered or worked part-time during high school as a teacher's aide, camp counselor, or tutor, she might have had a better understanding of the rewards and aggravations of working with children. If Dan had volunteered as a teenager to do summer office work, he might have learned that he was better suited to a less confining job.

Have you learned that there are some jobs that you definitely do not want? Work environments that you would not like? Certain types of work that are not for you? Jot down these items on the lines below:

____

____

____

____

____

GAINING EXPERIENCE THROUGH VOLUNTEER AND PART-TIME WORK

Places to work as a Body Worker

Small Machine Repairer

If you want to learn about repairing broken typewriters, adding machines and copying equipment, contact your local Volunteer Action Center. Many charitable organizations repair donated equipment for sale and can use people who are willing to learn to do careful work.

Firefighter

Call your local fire department and ask for suggestions for increasing your understanding of careers in the fire department. A volunteer fire department in your community or nearby may offer a volunteer training program.

Conservation and Forestry

The Isaac Walton League, Sierra Club, and Audubon Society publish helpful information and often offer student membership rates. Museums of natural science, botanic gardens, and zoos all offer work with plants and animals. It could be worth doing menial work to be near experts in the field. If you become knowledgeable, you might become a tour guide, explain displays to visiting groups of students, or be part of a conservation crew that will give you valuable experience.

Agriculture

Future Farmers of America and 4-H Clubs have many good activities. Some residential care facilities such as halfway houses encourage residents to have gardens and need volunteers to help with the programs. Summer work may be available on nearby farms as well.

Landscape Architect

Public gardens and park districts often use volunteers who can learn first-hand about specific needs of plants, shrubs, and trees for shade, sun, water, fertilizer, and special maintenance. In addition, much of the work of commercial landscape architects is done in spring and summer. Call early to line up a summer job.

Cook or Baker

Local Meals-on-Wheels programs deliver hot meals to disabled people. Volunteers are often used in the kitchen where the demands of volume cooking can be observed first-hand. You may also be able to get part-time jobs for either evenings or weekends in bakeries or institutional or restaurant kitchens.

Upholstery and Furniture Repair

Many organizations need help in repairing furniture. Contact your local Volunteer Action Center for information. Check the Yellow Pages of the telephone directory to locate businesses where you may be able to get part time work and training.

Places to work as an Investigator

Historian

Some libraries employ students to interview local residents as part of oral history projects. Museums likewise welcome volunteers and can give close exposure to the remains of the past. Historical societies also welcome student members.

Veterinarian

Convince a local veterinarian that you could be helpful cleaning cages, feeding animals, sorting medicines, and preparing examining rooms, and you will have a good opportunity to see the day-to-day work of animal health care. Animal shelters and the Humane Society will also welcome volunteers.

Optometrist

The Society for the Prevention of Blindness concerns itself with sight-saving projects. Volunteers help screen preschoolers for vision problems and use tutors and aids for their training centers for the blind.

Places to work as a Creative Artist

Architecture

Few volunteer responsibilities are available for high school students, but fifth year architectural graduate students can work as paraprofessionals in 90 Community Design Centers (CDC), many sponsored by the American Institute of Architects. These centers provide services to people who cannot afford to employ an architect for one small project, such as an addition to a private home. Related industries such as real estate, construction, landmark preservation groups, etc., may provide part-time work, either paid or as a volunteer.

Artists

Day care centers, day camps, Y's and community centers often need volunteer teachers to work with children in the arts. Hundreds of organizations sponsor boutiques or bazaars where individual creations can be exhibited and sold. Communicating a willingness to do any task at an art museum (filing, gift shop sales, dusting artifacts) offers contact with the work of other artists. A brief course in keyline and pasteup will provide students with a skill for part time work for commercial artists and designers.

Interior Design

Part-time work for a furniture store or a wholesale furniture showroom will allow you to observe how current styles are being used. It will also allow you to find out who the best interior designers are and what their work is like. With experience in the furniture show rooms, you may next be able to land a part-time job as an interior designer's helper.

Writer

To practice writing, volunteer to help with some organization's newsletter. Any volunteer experience which allows you to observe how writers work for a living will help you to make a more realistic career choice.

Fashion

Many department stores have a teen counsel where students can learn about fashion trends and design. Helping a buyer or window dresser, or even part-time sales clerking in a good store will give you useful information.

Advertising and Public Relations

Many community organizations need to be better known within a community. Emergency care agencies and hotlines should be known to people in the area they serve; senior citizens should be aware of the services available to them in their communities. Volunteer to type press releases and contact the local press about activities which should be publicized.

Some large hospitals offer volunteers the opportunity to work with public relations professionals on a variety of projects such as newsletters, press releases, photo arrangements and fund raising. Summer work is rare, but if you can stuff envelopes, type, or file, try the commercial agencies for a part time or temporary job.

Performing Arts

Recording for the Blind and the Braille Institute offer volunteer opportunities for performers to make records of recent books, plays, songs, magazine articles.

Many hospitals and convalescent homes have an unending stream of entertainers at Christmas but could use some diversion the rest of the year. Professional theatres, opera houses, and summer stock theatres, have apprenticeship programs in which the pay is low, and the waiting list is usually long. The Actors Equity office in any large city will be able to give you names and addresses of the theatres in your area. You should apply a year ahead of time. Get your name on the list, and keep calling and dropping by to remind them of your application until you get the job.

Places to work as a Service Worker

Counselor and Psychologist

Hotlines and telephone crisis services for teenagers employ teenagers themselves. Their training courses can be valuable in learning how to help people in crisis situations. Halfway houses and social clubs for former mental patients offer controlled situations ideal for the beginning volunteer.

Teacher

Working with children in educational or recreation programs sponsored by community, civic, and religious groups will give experience with normal children.

Organizations that help handicapped children also offer experience in rehabilitative education. Many public and private schools welcome teacher's aides and tutors on a regular basis. Day care centers may be a source of part-time work for after school hours.

Personnel

Youth Employment Services available in some communities try to place students in full or part-time jobs. Volunteers interview students, advise them on how to go about a job interview, and contact possible employers. If there is not a Youth Employment Service in your school, you may be able to start one with the help of a faculty advisor.

Librarian

Volunteers at hospitals are sometimes used to deliver books to shut-ins and patients, do storytelling for children, and assist in making displays, decorations and posters for the children's room. Part-time work may be available in your school library or a private or public library in the community.

Home Economist

The majority of home economists teach, so it would be wise to get some teaching experience. The Girl Scouts, Camp Fire Girls, and 4-H Clubs have cooking, nutrition, and clothing activities which welcome teenage volunteers. Many halfway houses teach domestic skills, and visiting nurse programs sometimes use volunteers to instruct people on maintaining their homes, adapting to uses of new foods, etc.

Health Services

Large hospitals often have a formal volunteer program for teenagers which gives a wide range of experience. Some work in emergency and physical therapy departments, gaining high school credit in work/study arrangements. Convalescent hospitals offer the opportunity to work with senior citizens and recuperating patients.

Public Contact Work

Hospitals provide opportunities to volunteers in admitting, and gift shops. Some have contact with patients while passing mail and delivering menus. Religious and public service organizations often have volunteer programs in hospitals. Choose a hospital you'd like to work in, and talk with the volunteer coordinator or the personnel department.

Places to work as a Persuader

Legal Professions

The Legal Aid Society and some public defender staffs use teenage volunteers or part-time workers to run errands, do clerical work, and answer telephones. The Office of Economic Opportunity and Consumer Affairs Bureau help volunteers and part-time workers learn about consumer laws while providing clerical assistance.

Politician

Many modern presidents began their careers in local politics. A great deal can be learned about campaigning by working door-to-door, phoning voters, stuffing envelopes, and passing flyers. Local politicians and school board and park district representatives often need help. The League of Women Voters keeps tabs on local government and operates an effective information service about government structures, representatives and issues. Membership is open to men and women over age 18. All political parties welcome volunteers; so do all candidates for office. Some paid positions are sometimes also available.

Salesperson

Part-time or summer work as a salesperson will allow you to try your hand at convincing others of the need to buy—whether you are selling candy, brushes, or real estate, you will find out if you can sell.

Places to work in the Data Detail

Banking

Some high schools have credit unions. Loans are made to depositors, interest is charged, and profit sharing is paid to shareholders. Information on starting a Credit Union at your school can be obtained from the National Credit Union Administration, Washington D.C. 02456. A part-time job in a bank will give you a chance to observe the various kinds of workers in their jobs.

Accountant

Every organization that collects dues and receives contributions needs a treasurer. Serving as a volunteer treasurer of an organization will allow you to practice the basics. You will need some educational background to get part-time accounting work.

Travel Agent

The Traveler's Aid Society offers students the opportunity to learn some of the problems facing travelers. The International Student Service is an organization that greets visiting students from other countries who want to sightsee before reaching their place of schooling. Contact travel agents in your community for part-time work, and to discuss training needs for the work.

Clerical Work

Virtually every public service organization needs clerical assistance. The United Fund, consumer bureaus, public health offices, and free clinics are but a few of the places which would welcome clerical help.

FIELD EXPERIENCE OBSERVATION SHEET

Select three organizations which might use volunteer or part-time help you can provide. Write the names, addresses, and phone numbers of the organizations on the sheet below. Phone them and ask to speak with the person in charge of personnel. Explain what you would like to do, and ask if work is available. If it is not, ask the person to give you any suggestions about other organizations to call, or other information you should have.

Name: ______________________________

Address: ______________________________

Contact: ______________________________

Observations: ______________________________

____

Name: ______________________________

Address: ______________________________

Contact: ______________________________

Observations: ______________________________

____

Name: ______________________________

Address: ______________________________

Contact: ______________________________

Observations: ______________________________

____

Name: ______________________________

Address: ______________________________

Contact: ______________________________

Observations: ______________________________

____

9. The Advice Interview

Reading about an occupation seldom gives enough motivation to cause someone to choose a career. The real thrust comes from personal encouragement, from talking with people who are enthusiastic about their work. It is important to locate and speak with people who work in fields that interest you.

Use family members, friends, and other contacts for introductions to people working in specific occupations. Explain that you are using a career program workbook to search out a career and that at this time you must interview people working in fields that you find attractive. Ask people to meet with you or to at least answer questions over the telephone. If the first people you ask refuse, keep trying. There are many people who enjoy talking about their jobs or helping others find direction.

Here are some questions worth asking:

How did you happen to choose this occupation?

What do you like best about it?

What do you like least?

What kind of people tend to do well in this kind of job?

Do you do the same thing all day long or is there variety?

Can you think of some particular event on your job that made you feel good? What was it?

What kinds of things happen on the job to make you angry or sad?

What are the opportunities for the future?

What kinds of problems does this industry have? labor? costs?

What do you see as the purposes, goals, and values that your employer serves?

What qualifications are needed to do the job? what training?

Can you recommend the names of people for me to talk to?

Who might hire me for an entry level job in this area once I get the qualifications?

POSSIBLE INTERROGATIONS

List names of people whom you could interview about jobs and careers.

Name	*Position*	*Special notes*

Whose job would you like most to have? Why?________________________________

____

____

What needs to be done to get that job?____________________________________

____

____

10. Research a Career

One of the greatest and most common career mistakes is not choosing a career because you are unaware that it exists. Any library contains many tools for investigation that can be used to uncover interesting career possibilities.

Excellent Reference Books

Dictionary of Occupational Titles. As big as a telephone book from a major city, the D.O.T. is the greatest source of occupational information. It lists over 20,000 job titles and describes the occupations by physical demands, individual working conditions, interest, educational requirements, and vocational preparation. A code number describes workers' involvement with information, people and things.

Occupational Outlook Handbook. Less confusing to use than the D.O.T., this book describes the employment outlook, work, required training, earnings and working conditions for 700 occupations.

Encyclopedia of Career and Vocational Guidance. This source provides specific information on salaries, and also lists educational requirements, advancement possibilities, and specific demands for over 650 occupations.

Occupational Guidance. This easy-to-read eight-volume set describes the work, earnings, history, working conditions, hours, abilities, requirements, temperament needed, education, attractive and unattractive features, suggested high school courses, and even gives questions to test your interest in specific fields.

The Card Catalog

Look under individual occupations that interest you to locate books which you may take home. For instance, look under *A* for aviation, *O* for office work.

The Vertical File

Many libraries store excellent pamphlets on individual careers under *C* in the vertical files. You may have to ask the librarian to get materials from the vertical files.

Professional Journals and Directories

Almost every career field has a special magazine or a professional journal which gives updates on the special situations facing people in that occupation. Articles often contain names of people to contact directly about employment. Many such journals also list job openings.

Libraries reference departments also have directories which list employers in specific industries. The three largest directories are as follows:

Dun and Bradstreet Million Dollar Directories (3 volumes: volume lists firms with net worth over $1.2 million; volume 2, firms with net worth between $900 thousand and $1.2 million; volume 3, firms with net worth between $500 and $900 thousand. Gives locations, products, executives' names, number of employees.): Dun and Bradstreet, 99 Church St. New York, NY 10004.

Standard & Poor's Register of Corporations Directors and Executives (400,000 key executives in 38,000 leading companies cross-referenced by product and company location. Includes home addresses of executives plus title and duties.): Standard & Poor's Corp., 25 Broadway, New York, NY 10004.

11. The Composite Picture

Crime witnesses frequently work with police artists in drafting composite pictures of suspects. At this point you can assemble all the clues from your career search and draw a composite picture of the career that would make you happy. Go back over the exercises in this book and summarize what you have learned about the job that will make you happiest.

Your dream job

Strongest skills

Rewards that will make you happy

Job characteristics you don't want

Job characteristics you do want

Kinds of co-workers you want

Important, ultimate life goals

Prime job possibilities so far

Use additional paper to write out all your thoughts on these questions. Remember, too, that all of these thoughts will change during your lifetime to some degree; this is your job needs profile for right now, and the foreseeable future—you'll want to assess your needs and preferences again, later on, perhaps many times.

12. The Career Finder

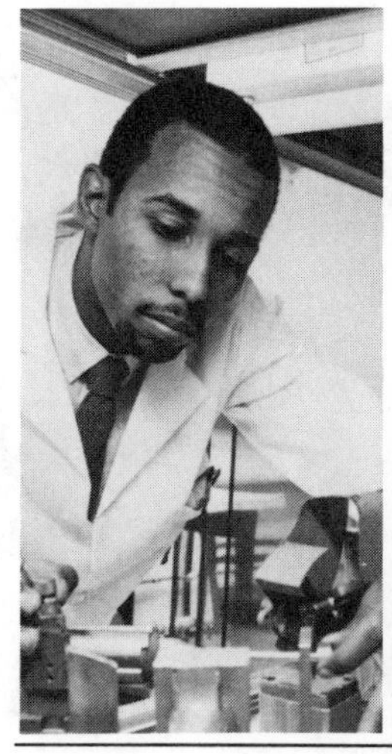

The Career Finder on the following pages gives you an extensive checklist of information about many kinds of jobs and their characteristics.

Each job listing is coded for the type of job group with a two-letter code. This is the same letter code you have used in your activity and work sheets previously.

Footnotes, indicated by an asterisk following job titles in the Career Finder list, appear after the last page of the Career Finder, page 62.

Each job listing is followed by numbered columns which provide information about the job's requirements or characteristics. The list on the following page is your key to using the numbered columns.

The estimated number of workers in the kinds of jobs at present, the projected openings in the kinds of jobs each year, and the description of the employment picture for the job areas in the future are also included.

25 COMMON JOB SKILLS AND CHARACTERISTICS

These 25 job skills and characteristics are keyed to the Career Finder on the following pages. An *X* appears in the numbered column on the Career Finder whenever the skill or characteristic is related to the specific job.

1. High school diploma generally required.
2. Technical school or apprenticeship. Some form of non-degree post high school training required.
3. Junior college degree. Requires Associate in Arts degree.
4. College degree. Requires at least a bachelor's degree. (C = 4-year degree; G = 1 or more years graduate work or first professional degree.)
5. Jobs widely scattered. Jobs are located in most areas of the United States.
6. Jobs concentrated in one or a few geographical locations.
7. Works with things: Jobs generally require manual skills.
8. Works with ideas. Uses one's intellect to solve problems.
9. Helps people. Assists people in a helping relationship.
10. Works with people. Job generally requires pleasing personality and ability to get along with others.
11. Able to see physical results of work. Work produces a tangible product.
12. Opportunity for self-expression. Freedom to use one's own ideas.
13. Works as part of a team. Interacts with fellow employees in performing work.
14. Works independently. Requires self-discipline and ability to organize.
15. Work is closely supervised. Job performance and work standards controlled.
16. Directs activities of others. Work entails supervisory responsibilities.
17. Generally confined to work area. Physically located at one work setting.
18. Overtime or shift work required. Work hours other than normal daytime shifts.
19. Exposed to weather or is subjected to temperature extremes.
20. High level of responsibility. Requires making key decisions involving property, finances, or human safety and welfare.
21. Requires physical stamina. Must be in physical condition for continued lifting, standing, and walking.
22. Works with details. Works with technical data, numbers, or written materials on a continuous basis.
23. Repetitious work. Performs the same task on a continuous basis.
24. Motivates others. Must be able to influence others.
25. Competitive. Competes with other people on the job.

Type of Work and Coworkers	Occupation	1 High School diploma	2 Technical school or apprenticeship	3 Junior college	4 College degree	5 Jobs widely scattered	6 Jobs concentrated in locations	7 Work with things	8 Work with ideas	9 Help people	10 Work with people	11 Able to see physical results of work	12 Opportunity for self-expression	13 Work as part of a team	14 Work independently	15 Work closely supervised	16 Direct activity of others	17 Generally confined to work area	18 Overtime or shift work required	19 Outdoors	20 High level of responsibility	21 Requires physical stamina	22 Work with detail	23 Repetitious work	24 Motivate others	25 Competitive	Estimated Employment – 1980	Range of Possible Change in Employment (Hundreds) 1980-1990	Employment Prospects
FOUNDRY OCCUPATIONS																													
BI**	Patternmakers	X	A			X		X				X		X		X		X					X				3,000	6 to 9	Employment expected to grow more slowly than average. Use of durable metal patterns will offset increases in foundry productions.
BI	Molders*		A			X						X		X		X		X					X				24,000	6 to 9	Below average. Large demand likely for metal castings.
BI	Coremakers		A			X		X				X		X			X					X	X	X			6,200	6 to 9	Employment expected to increase more slowly than average as growing use of machine coremaking limits the need for additional workers.

MACHINING OCCUPATIONS

Type of Work and Coworkers	Occupation	1	2	3	4	5	6	7	8	9	10	11	12	13	14	15	16	17	18	19	20	21	22	23	24	25	Estimated Employment – 1980	Range of Possible Change in Employment (Hundreds) 1980-1990	Employment Prospects
BI	All-round machinists*		A			X		X				X			X			X				X	X	X			303,000	16 to 29	Employment expected to increase about as fast as average due to growing demand for machined metal parts. Many openings likely in maintenance shops of manufacturing plants.
BI	Instrument makers*	X	A				X	X				X		X			X						X				43,000	18 to 33	Average. Laborsaving innovations may limit growth.
BI	Machine tool operators*		X			X		X				X			X			X				X	X	X			1,020,000	18 to 21	Average
BI	Setup Workers*	X	A				X	X				X			X			X				X	X				93,000	21 to 30	Average, however advances in tool-making may limit growth.

TYPE OF WORK AND COWORKERS	OCCUPATION	1 High School diploma	2 Technical school or apprenticeship	3 Junior college	4 College degree	5 Jobs widely scattered	6 Jobs concentrated in locations	7 Work with things	8 Work with ideas	9 Help people	10 Work with people	11 Able to see physical results of work	12 Opportunity for self-expression	13 Work as part of a team	14 Work independently	15 Work closely supervised	16 Direct activity of others	17 Generally confined to work area	18 Overtime or shift work required	19 Outdoors	20 High level of responsibility	21 Requires physical stamina	22 Work with detail	23 Repetitious work	24 Motivate others	25 Competitive	ESTIMATED EMPLOYMENT - 1980	RANGE OF POSSIBLE CHANGE IN EMPLOYMENT (HUNDREDS) 1980-1990	EMPLOYMENT PROSPECTS
MACHINING OCCUPATIONS																													
BI	Tool-and-die makers*		A				X	X				X			X	X		X	X				X	X			166,000	8 to 24	Employment expected to grow more slowly than average as advances in tool making processes limit growth. Because of a shortage of experienced workers, excellent job opportunities expected.
PRINTING OCCUPATIONS																													
BC	Compositors	X	A				X	X						X		X		X	X				X	X			128,000	−2 to 10	Declining due to high-speed phototypesetting and typesetting computers. Best prospects for graduates of professional printing technology courses.
BC	Lithographers	X	A				X	X						X		X		X	X				X	X			45,000	31 to 42	Employment expected to increase faster than average in resonse to continued growth of offset printing. Best job prospects for graduates of postsecondary school programs in printing technology.
BD	Photoengravers	X	A				X	X				X		X				X	X				X	X			10,000	−5 to −3	Declining because of switch from letterpress to offset printing.
BD	Electrotypers and stereotypers	X	A				X	X				X		X		X		X	X				X	X			1,900	−42 to −46	Declining due to greater use of offset printing and other laborsaving equipment.
BI	Printing press operators and assistants*	X	A				X	X						X					X			X					178,000	9 to 17	Slowing as faster and more efficient presses limit growth.

TYPE OF WORK AND COWORKERS	OCCUPATION	High School diploma	Technical school or apprenticeship	Junior college	College degree	Jobs widely scattered	Jobs concentrated in locations	Work with things	Work with ideas	Help people	Work with people	Able to see physical results of work	Opportunity for self-expression	Work as part of a team	Work independently	Work closely supervised	Direct activity of others	Generally confined to work area	Overtime or shift work required	Outdoors	High level of responsibility	Requires physical stamina	Work with detail	Repetitious work	Motivate others	Competitive	ESTIMATED EMPLOYMENT – 1980	RANGE OF POSSIBLE CHANGE IN EMPLOYMENT (HUNDREDS) 1980-1990	EMPLOYMENT PROSPECTS
		1	2	3	4	5	6	7	8	9	10	11	12	13	14	15	16	17	18	19	20	21	22	23	24	25			
PRINTING OCCUPATIONS																													
BC	Bookbinders and binder workers*	X	A			X		X				X			X			X						X			117,000	– 4 to – 5	Slowing due to increasing mechanization of bindery operations.
OTHER INDUSTRIAL PRODUCTION AND RELATED OCCUPATIONS																													
BD	Assemblers					X	X							X		X		X						X			1,670,000	19 to 31	Increasing due to growing demand for consumer products and industrial equipment. Economic changes and national defense spending often affect job opportunities.
BD	Automobile painters*		X			X		X				X			X	X		X						X			41,000	38 to 44	Employment expected to increase faster than average due to growing number of vehicles and traffic accidents.
PB	Blue-collar workers supervisors	X	(1)	(1)	(1)	(1)					X			X		X	X		X		X						1,300,000	16 to 25	Employment expected to increase about as fast as average. Large part of increase in nonmanufacturing industries.
CLERICAL OCCUPATIONS																													
DI	Bookkeepers and accounting clerks	X				X								X		X		X					X	X			1,700,000	15 to 24	Increasing use of bookkeeping machines and electronic computers will limit growth. Due to high replacement needs, job opportunities are expected to be numerous.
DI	Cashiers					X					X				X	X		X					X	X			1,600,000	28 to 36	Widespread adoption of automatic checkout systems could slow future growth.

TYPE OF WORK AND COWORKERS	OCCUPATION	1 High School diploma	2 Technical school or apprenticeship	3 Junior college	4 College degree	5 Jobs widely scattered	6 Jobs concentrated in locations	7 Work with things	8 Work with ideas	9 Help people	10 Work with people	11 Able to see physical results of work	12 Opportunity for self-expression	13 Work as part of a team	14 Work independently	15 Work closely supervised	16 Direct activity of others	17 Generally confined to work area	18 Overtime or shift work required	19 Outdoors	20 High level of responsibility	21 Requires physical stamina	22 Work with detail	23 Repetitious work	24 Motivate others	25 Competitive	ESTIMATED EMPLOYMENT – 1980	RANGE OF POSSIBLE CHANGE IN EMPLOYMENT (HUNDREDS) 1980-1990	EMPLOYMENT PROSPECTS
CLERICAL OCCUPATIONS																													
DP	Hotel front office clerks	X				X				X	X				X			X	X				X				80,000	15 to 30	Employment expected to grow as fast as average. The use of computerized reservation systems may limit growth.
DB	Typists	X				X		X				X			X	X		X					X	X			1,100,000	18 to 25	Employment expected to grow as fast as average as business expansion increases the amount of paperwork. Replacement needs will remain high. Demand particularly strong for typists who can handle a variety of office duties and operate word-processing equipment.
DB	Computer-operating personnel	X	X			X		X						X		X		X	X				X	X					Average growth in employment of console and peripheral equipment operators expected to rise faster than average as use of computers expands. Employment of keypunch operators expected to decline, however, due to more efficient direct data entry techniques.
ID	Programmers	X	(1)	(1)	(1)	X			X					X			X	X					X				228,000	49 to 60	Employment expected to grow much faster than average as computer usage expands, particularly in accounting, business management, data processing services, and research and development. Brightest prospects for college graduates with degree in computer science or related field.
PI	Systems analysts				X	X			X					X									X				205,000	68 to 80	Excellent prospects for graduates of computer-related curriculums.

Column key (types of work and coworkers): 1 High School diploma; 2 Technical school or apprenticeship; 3 Junior college; 4 College degree; 5 Jobs widely scattered; 6 Jobs concentrated in locations; 7 Work with things; 8 Work with ideas; 9 Help people; 10 Work with people; 11 Able to see physical results of work; 12 Opportunity for self-expression; 13 Work as part of a team; 14 Work independently; 15 Work closely supervised; 16 Direct activity of others; 17 Generally confined to work area; 18 Overtime or shift work required; 19 Outdoors; 20 High level of responsibility; 21 Requires physical stamina; 22 Work with detail; 23 Repetitious work; 24 Motivate others; 25 Competitive

TYPE OF WORK AND COWORKERS	OCCUPATION	1	2	3	4	5	6	7	8	9	10	11	12	13	14	15	16	17	18	19	20	21	22	23	24	25	ESTIMATED EMPLOYMENT – 1980	RANGE OF POSSIBLE CHANGE IN EMPLOYMENT (HUNDREDS) 1980-1990	EMPLOYMENT PROSPECTS
BANKING OCCUPATIONS																													
DI	Bank clerks	X			X	X				X	x				X		X				X		X				1,000,000	26 to 32	Employment expected to grow faster than average as banking services expand. Employment growth will differ markedly among individual clerical occupations.
PD	Bank officers and managers	X				X								X		X		X					X	X			400,000	26 to 33	Employment expected to grow faster than average as banks expand services. Competition for managerial positions likely to stiffen.
DP	Bank tellers	X				X				X	X				X	X		X					X				480,000	25 to 29	Employment expected to grow faster than average as banks expand services. Opportunities for both full-time and part-time positions should be good.
INSURANCE OCCUPATIONS																													
ID	Actuaries				X		X		X				X		X			X					X	X			8,000	40 to 48	Employment expected to rise faster than average as insurance sales increase and insurance companies introduce new forms of insurance and reevaluate existing health and pension plans.
ID	Claim representatives	X		(1)	(1)	X				X	X				X				X				X				210,000	39 to 43	Employment expected to grow faster than average due to increasing insurance claims.
PI	Underwriters				X		X		X														X				325,000	22 to 29	Employment expected to grow as fast as average as insurance sales expand.

ADMINISTRATIVE AND RELATED OCCUPATIONS

TYPE OF WORK AND COWORKERS	OCCUPATION	1 High School diploma	2 Technical school or apprenticeship	3 Junior college	4 College degree	5 Jobs widely scattered	6 Jobs concentrated in locations	7 Work with things	8 Work with ideas	9 Help people	10 Work with people	11 Able to see physical results of work	12 Opportunity for self-expression	13 Work as part of a team	14 Work independently	15 Work closely supervised	16 Direct activity of others	17 Generally confined to work area	18 Overtime or shift work required	19 Outdoors	20 High level of responsibility	21 Requires physical stamina	22 Work with detail	23 Repetitious work	24 Motivate others	25 Competitive	ESTIMATED EMPLOYMENT – 1980	RANGE OF POSSIBLE CHANGE IN EMPLOYMENT (HUNDREDS) 1980-1990	EMPLOYMENT PROSPECTS
D1	Accountants				X	X			X						X			X					X	X			900,000	25 to 34	Employment expected to increase faster than average as managers rely more on accounting information to make business decisions. College graduates will be in greater demand than applicants who lack this training.
CP	Advertising workers				X		X		X				X	X					X						X	X	100,000	(3)	Employment expected to grow due to increased number of products and services advertised.
PD	Buyers				X	X			X						X		X				X		X		X	X	150,000	20 to 27	Average. Keen competition anticipated because merchandising attracts numbers of college graduates.
PD	City managers				X	X			X	X				X			X				X		X				3,300	1 to 2	Competition will be keen, even for persons with graduate degrees in public administration.
SP	College student personnel workers				X	X				X	X			X			X				X				X		55,000	(3)	Competition for jobs expected due to tighter budgets in public and private colleges.
DI	Credit managers	X				X			X						X		X	X			X		X	X			55,000	0	Employment expected to grow more slowly than average as centralization of credit operations increases.

TYPE OF WORK AND COWORKERS	OCCUPATION	1 High School diploma	2 Technical school or apprenticeship	3 Junior college	4 College degree	5 Jobs widely scattered	6 Jobs concentrated in locations	7 Work with things	8 Work with ideas	9 Help people	10 Work with people	11 Able to see physical results of work	12 Opportunity for self-expression	13 Work as part of a team	14 Work independently	15 Work closely supervised	16 Direct activity of others	17 Generally confined to work area	18 Overtime or shift work required	19 Outdoors	20 High level of responsibility	21 Requires physical stamina	22 Work with detail	23 Repetitious work	24 Motivate others	25 Competitive	ESTIMATED EMPLOYMENT – 1980	RANGE OF POSSIBLE CHANGE IN EMPLOYMENT (HUNDREDS) 1980-1990	EMPLOYMENT PROSPECTS
ADMINISTRATIVE AND RELATED OCCUPATIONS																													
PI	Lawyers				+	X			X	X			X		X				X		X		X		X	X	425,000	25 to 39	Keen competition likely for salaried positions. Best prospects for establishing new practices will be in small towns and expanding suburbs, although starting a practice will remain risky and expensive.
IP	Marketing research analysts				X		X		X					X									X			X	29,300	(3)	Best opportunities for applicants with graduate training in marketing research or statistics.
SIP	Personnel and labor relations workers				X	X				X	X			X			X				X		X				178,000	15 to 22	Average as employers seek to raise productivity through training and development and other employee benefit programs. Keen competition for jobs in labor relations.
PC	Public relations workers				X		X		X				X	X					X				X		X	X	87,000	18 to 26	Competition for jobs likely to be keen especially during economic downturns.
ID	Purchasing agents				X	X			X						X		X				X		X		X	X	172,000	16 to 24	Excellent job opportunities for persons with master's degrees in business administration.
SERVICE OCCUPATIONS																													
SP	Bartenders					X				X	X				X			X	X								382,000	19 to 26	Average

Type of Work and Coworkers	Occupation	1 High School diploma	2 Technical school or apprenticeship	3 Junior college	4 College degree	5 Jobs widely scattered	6 Jobs concentrated in locations	7 Work with things	8 Work with ideas	9 Help people	10 Work with people	11 Able to see physical results of work	12 Opportunity for self-expression	13 Work as part of a team	14 Work independently	15 Work closely supervised	16 Direct activity of others	17 Generally confined to work area	18 Overtime or shift work required	19 Outdoors	20 High level of responsibility	21 Requires physical stamina	22 Work with detail	23 Repetitious work	24 Motivate others	25 Competitive	Estimated Employment – 1980	Range of Possible Change in Employment (Hundreds) 1980-1990	Employment Prospects
SERVICE OCCUPATIONS																													
BI	Cooks and chefs		X	X		X		X		X				X			X		X								1,100,000	22 to 28	Employment expected to increase as fast as average as population grows and people dine out more. Most starting jobs are available in small restaurants, school cafeterias, and other eating places where food preparation is relatively simple.
BD	Hotel housekeepers and assistants					X				X					X		X						X				18,000	23 to 39	Employment expected to grow faster than average. Best opportunities in newly built hotels and motels.
BP	Meatcutters*		X A			X		X							X			X				X		X			190,000	11 to 18	Declining because of practice of cutting and wrapping meat for several stores at one location.
BP	Waiters and waitresses					X				X	X			X					X			X					1,700,000	21 to 28	Average.
PERSONAL SERVICE OCCUPATIONS																													
BP	Barbers		X			X				X	X	X						X						X			112,000	7 to 22	Most openings will result from replacement needs. Better opportunities for hairstylists than for conventional barbers.
BP	Bellhops and bell captains					X				X	X				X				X			X					21,000	5 to 18	Little change in employment expected. Best opportunities in motels, small hotels and resort areas open only part of the year.

TYPE OF WORK AND COWORKERS	OCCUPATION	1 High School diploma	2 Technical school or apprenticeship	3 Junior college	4 College degree	5 Jobs widely scattered	6 Jobs concentrated in locations	7 Work with things	8 Work with ideas	9 Help people	10 Work with people	11 Able to see physical results of work	12 Opportunity for self-expression	13 Work as part of a team	14 Work independently	15 Work closely supervised	16 Direct activity of others	17 Generally confined to work area	18 Overtime or shift work required	19 Outdoors	20 High level of responsibility	21 Requires physical stamina	22 Work with detail	23 Repetitious work	24 Motivate others	25 Competitive	ESTIMATED EMPLOYMENT – 1980	RANGE OF POSSIBLE CHANGE IN EMPLOYMENT (HUNDREDS) 1980-1990	EMPLOYMENT PROSPECTS
PERSONAL SERVICE OCCUPATIONS																													
SC	Cosmetologists		T			X				X	X	X						X									515,000	14 to 29	Employment expected to grow about as fast as average as demand for beauty shop services rises. Opportunities for part-time work should be very good.
IS	FBI special agents*				G		X			X	X			X					X		X	X	X				8,000	(3)	Rising as FBI responsibilities grow. Traditionally low turnover rate.
BS	Firefighters*	X				X		X		X				X					X	X		X					275,000	17 to 19	Employment expected to increase about as fast as average as need for fire protection grows and professionals replace volunteers. Keen competition for jobs in urban areas; better opportunities in smaller communities.
BS	Guards*					X									X				X		X	X					650,000	23 to 34	Best opportunities in guard and security agencies and in nightshift jobs.
BS	Police officers*	X				X				X	X				X	X			X	X	X	X	X				495,000	17 to 19	Best prospects for applicants with college training in law enforcement.
BS	State police officers*	X				X				X	X				X	X			X	X	X	X	X				55,000	13 to 15	Tight budgets will cause competition for jobs in most states.
ID	Health and regulatory inspectors (government)*		(1)	(1)	(1)	X			X						X						X		X		X		112,000	12-14	Below average.

TYPE OF WORK AND COWORKERS	OCCUPATION	High School diploma	Technical school or apprenticeship	Junior college	College degree	Jobs widely scattered	Jobs concentrated in locations	Work with things	Work with ideas	Help people	Work with people	Able to see physical results of work	Opportunity for self-expression	Work as part of a team	Work independently	Work closely supervised	Direct activity of others	Generally confined to work area	Overtime or shift work required	Outdoors	High level of responsibility	Requires physical stamina	Work with detail	Repetitious work	Motivate others	Competitive	ESTIMATED EMPLOYMENT – 1980	RANGE OF POSSIBLE CHANGE IN EMPLOYMENT (HUNDREDS) 1980-1990	EMPLOYMENT PROSPECTS
		1	2	3	4	5	6	7	8	9	10	11	12	13	14	15	16	17	18	19	20	21	22	23	24	25			
PERSONAL SERVICE OCCUPATIONS																													
IB	Construction inspectors (government)*	X	T			X			X						X					X	X	X	X				48,000	26 to 28	Best opportunities for college graduates and persons experienced as carpenters, electricians, or plumbers. Rising concern for safe construction will result in better than average job prospects.
OTHER SERVICE OCCUPATIONS																													
BD	Mail carriers					X		X		X					X					X		X					250,000	–18	Employment expected to decline due to rising productivity and to falling mail volume as businesses increase their use of electronic communications and private delivery systems.
DP	Telephone operators	X				X		X		X					X			X	X								340,000	14 to 15	Declining due to increased direct dialing and technological improvements.
EDUCATION AND RELATED OCCUPATIONS																													
TEACHING OCCUPATIONS																													
SP	Kindergarten and elementary school teachers				+	X			X	X	X		X		X		X		X		X			X	X		1,600,000	18 to 19	Employment expected to grow as fast as average. Job prospects may improve in the late 1980s due to rising enrollments in lower grades. Outlook for qualified elementary school teachers is likely to be good unless the number of job seekers increases.

	Occupation	1 High School diploma	2 Technical school or apprenticeship	3 Junior college	4 College degree	5 Jobs widely scattered	6 Jobs concentrated in locations	7 Work with things	8 Work with ideas	9 Help people	10 Work with people	11 Able to see physical results of work	12 Opportunity for self-expression	13 Work as part of a team	14 Work independently	15 Work closely supervised	16 Direct activity of others	17 Generally confined to work area	18 Overtime or shift work required	19 Outdoors	20 High level of responsibility	21 Requires physical stamina	22 Work with detail	23 Repetitious work	24 Motivate others	25 Competitive	Estimated Employment – 1980	Range of Possible Change in Employment (Hundreds) 1980-1990	Employment Prospects
EDUCATION AND RELATED OCCUPATIONS																													
TEACHING OCCUPATIONS																													
SP	Secondary school teachers				+	X			X	X	X		X		X		X		X		X				X		1,237,000	–14	Keen competition expected due to sharply declining enrollments coupled with a continued oversupply of new college graduates qualified to teach. Generally, favorable opportunities will exist for persons qualified to teach special education, vocational subjects, mathematics, and the natural and physical sciences.
SI	College and university faculty				+	X			X	X	X		X		X		X								X		691,000[5]	–9	Employment expected to decline due to decreasing enrollments and budgetary constraints. Keen competition in all but a few disciplines, and many of the available openings will be part-time or short term. Good job prospects for engineering and computer science faculty.
LIBRARY OCCUPATIONS																													
DI	Librarians				+	X				X					X				X				X				135,000	3 to 5	Little change expected in employment in school, public, and academic libraries due to declining enrollments and budget constraints. Keen competition for jobs. Best opportunities for librarians with scientific or technical qualifications.
AD	Library technicians and assistants		T			X				X				X					X				X				154,000	3 to 4	Little change expected in employment. Best job prospects in special libraries.

SALES OCCUPATIONS

TYPE OF WORK AND COWORKERS	OCCUPATION	1 High School diploma	2 Technical school or apprenticeship	3 Junior college	4 College degree	5 Jobs widely scattered	6 Jobs concentrated in locations	7 Work with things	8 Work with ideas	9 Help people	10 Work with people	11 Able to see physical results of work	12 Opportunity for self-expression	13 Work as part of a team	14 Work independently	15 Work closely supervised	16 Direct activity of others	17 Generally confined to work area	18 Overtime or shift work required	19 Outdoors	20 High level of responsibility	21 Requires physical stamina	22 Work with detail	23 Repetitious work	24 Motivate others	25 Competitive	ESTIMATED EMPLOYMENT – 1980	RANGE OF POSSIBLE CHANGE IN EMPLOYMENT (HUNDREDS) 1980-1990	EMPLOYMENT PROSPECTS
PI	Automobile parts counter workers	X				X		X		X	X				X												105,000	18 to 28	Better than average due to increasing demand for new accessories and replacement parts.
S PI	Automobile sales workers	X				X				X	X				X				X					X	X	X	157,000	26 to 36	Employment expected to grow faster than average as demand for automobiles increases. Job openings may fluctuate, however, because sales are affected by changing economic conditions.
PI	Manufacturers and sales workers				+	X				X	X				X				X		X		X		X	X	440,000	15 to 24	Employment expected to grow about as fast as average. Good opportunities for persons with product knowledge and sales ability.
CP	Models						X				X			X					X			X				X	60,000	(3)	Better than average due to rising advertising expenditures and greater sales of clothing and accessories. Because occupaton is so small and the glamour of modeling attracts many, competition should be keen.
PD	Real estate agents and brokers	X	T			X				X	X				X				X		X		X		X	X	580,000	34 to 46	Highly competitive. Best prospects for college graduates and transferees from other sales jobs.
PI	Retail trade sales workers					X				X	X				X				X						X	X	3,300,300	19 to 27	High turnover should create excellent opportunities for full-time, part-time and temporary work.

TYPE OF WORK AND COWORKERS	OCCUPATION	1 High School diploma	2 Technical school or apprenticeship	3 Junior college	4 College degree	5 Jobs widely scattered	6 Jobs concentrated in locations	7 Work with things	8 Work with ideas	9 Help people	10 Work with people	11 Able to see physical results of work	12 Opportunity for self-expression	13 Work as part of a team	14 Work independently	15 Work closely supervised	16 Direct activity of others	17 Generally confined to work area	18 Overtime or shift work required	19 Outdoors	20 High level of responsibility	21 Requires physical stamina	22 Work with detail	23 Repetitious work	24 Motivate others	25 Competitive	ESTIMATED EMPLOYMENT – 1980	RANGE OF POSSIBLE CHANGE IN EMPLOYMENT (HUNDREDS) 1980-1990	EMPLOYMENT PROSPECTS
SALES OCCUPATIONS																													
PB	Route drivers					X				X	X				X				X	X		X			X		200,000	20 to 30	Several thousand openings will result annually from replacement needs. Best opportunities for applicants who have sales experience and good driving records.
PD	Securities sales workers				+	X			X	X	X				X				X			X			X	X	63,000	26 to 44	Employment expected to grow faster than average as economic growth and rising personal incomes increase the funds available for installing private security systems.
PD	Travel agents		T					X			X	X				X			X	X							52,000	43 to 52	Highly competitive. Opportunities sensitive to economic changes.
PD	Wholesale trade	X				X				X	X				X				X				X		X	X	1,100,000	19 to 30	Good opportunities for persons with product knowledge and sales ability.
CONSTRUCTION OCCUPATIONS																													
BD	Bricklayers, stonemasons, and marble setters*		A			X		X				X		X						X		X					154,000	39 to 50	Job openings should be plentiful except during economic downturns.
BD	Carpenters*		X			X		X				X		X						X		X					970,000	18 to 27	Average.
BD	Cement masons and terrazzo workers*		X			X		X				X		X			X		X	X		X					113,000	37 to 47	Better than average due to growing construction activity and greater use of concrete as a building material.

CONSTRUCTION OCCUPATIONS

TYPE OF WORK AND COWORKERS	OCCUPATION	1 High School diploma	2 Technical school or apprenticeship	3 Junior college	4 College degree	5 Jobs widely scattered	6 Jobs concentrated in locations	7 Work with things	8 Work with ideas	9 Help people	10 Work with people	11 Able to see physical results of work	12 Opportunity for self-expression	13 Work as part of a team	14 Work independently	15 Work closely supervised	16 Direct activity of others	17 Generally confined to work area	18 Overtime or shift work required	19 Outdoors	20 High level of responsibility	21 Requires physical stamina	22 Work with detail	23 Repetitious work	24 Motivate others	25 Competitive	ESTIMATED EMPLOYMENT – 1980	RANGE OF POSSIBLE CHANGE IN EMPLOYMENT (HUNDREDS) 1980-1990	EMPLOYMENT PROSPECTS
BD	Construction laborers*					X		X						X		X			X	X		X		X			1,000,000	22 to 32	Employment expected to grow about as fast as average due to increasing construction activity. Job openings should be plentiful except during economic downturns.
BI	Electricians		A			X		X				X		X						X		X					560,000	20 to 28	Average, as more electricians are needed to install electrical fixtures and wiring in new and renovated buildings.
BI	Elevator constructors*					X		X				X		X								X					17,500	17 to 23	Better than average as number of high-rise apartments and commercial buildings grows.
BD	Floor covering installers		X			X		X				X			X							X					106,000	21[2]	Average. Best opportunities for those able to install carpeting and resilient flooring.
BD	Glaziers*	X	A			X		X				X			X					X		X					14,000	20 to 25	Average as popularity of glass in building design continues.
BD	Insulation workers*		X			X		X				X			X			X				X		X			45,400	31 to 40	Better than average as energy saving insulation is installed in homes and businesses.
BD	Ironworkers*	X						X				X		X								X		X			116,000	19 to 26	Employment expected to increase as fast as average due to growing demand for office and industrial buildings, transmission towers, and other structures.

TYPE OF WORK AND COWORKERS	OCCUPATION	High School diploma	Technical school or apprenticeship	Junior college	College degree	Jobs widely scattered	Jobs concentrated in locations	Work with things	Work with ideas	Help people	Work with people	Able to see physical results of work	Opportunity for self-expression	Work as part of a team	Work independently	Work closely supervised	Direct activity of others	Generally confined to work area	Overtime or shift work required	Outdoors	High level of responsibility	Requires physical stamina	Work with detail	Repetitious work	Motivate others	Competitive	ESTIMATED EMPLOYMENT – 1980	RANGE OF POSSIBLE CHANGE IN EMPLOYMENT (HUNDREDS) 1980-1990	EMPLOYMENT PROSPECTS
		1	2	3	4	5	6	7	8	9	10	11	12	13	14	15	16	17	18	19	20	21	22	23	24	25			
CONSTRUCTION OCCUPATIONS																													
BD	Operating Engineers (construction machinery operators)	X	T			X		X				X			X					X	X	X					270,000	15 to 28	Employment expected to grow as fast as average due to increasing construction activity. Job opportunities should be plentiful except during economic downturns.
BS	Painters*		X			X		X				X			X							X					382,000	14 to 25	Average.
BS	Paperhangers*		X			X		X				X			X							X					21,000	16 to 28	Better than average as populatiry of wallpaper rises.
BD	Plasterers		X			X		X				X		X								X					24,000	9 to 17	Employment will grow more slowly than average as drywall materials are used in place of plaster.
BI	Plumbers and pipefitters		A			X		X				X			X							X					407,000	20 to 28	Employment expected to grow about as fast as average as a result of increased construction activity and the need to repair and modernize existing plumbing and piping.
BI	Roofers*		X			X		X				X			X					X		X					113,000	15 to 24	Employment expected to grow as fast as average as a result of new construction and the need to repair existing roofs. Demand for damp-proofing and waterproofing also will stimulate employment.
BD	Sheet metal workers	X	A			X		X				X		X				X				X					108,000	20 to 26	Average due to need for air conditioning and heating ducts and other sheet metal products.

TYPE OF WORK AND COWORKERS	OCCUPATION	1 High School diploma	2 Technical school or apprenticeship	3 Junior college	4 College degree	5 Jobs widely scattered	6 Jobs concentrated in locations	7 Work with things	8 Work with ideas	9 Help people	10 Work with people	11 Able to see physical results of work	12 Opportunity for self-expression	13 Work as part of a team	14 Work independently	15 Work closely supervised	16 Direct activity of others	17 Generally confined to work area	18 Overtime or shift work required	19 Outdoors	20 High level of responsibility	21 Requires physical stamina	22 Work with detail	23 Repetitious work	24 Motivate others	25 Competitive	ESTIMATED EMPLOYMENT - 1980	RANGE OF POSSIBLE CHANGE IN EMPLOYMENT (HUNDREDS) 1980-1990	EMPLOYMENT PROSPECTS
CONSTRUCTION OCCUPATIONS																													
BD	Tilesetters		A			X		X				X			X			X				X					20,000	36 to 48	Employment expected to increase faster than average as tile is increasingly used in new kitchens, bathrooms, hallways, and recreation areas.
AIR TRANSPORTATION OCCUPATIONS																													
ID	Air traffic controllers	X	T				X		X					X			X	X	X		X		X				29,000	16 to 19	Best opportunities for college graduates with experience as controller pilots or navigators.
BI	Airplane mechanics*	X	T				X	X						X						X	X		X				110,000	40 to 50	Good opportunities in general aviation; keen competition for airline jobs; opportunities in Federal Government depending upon defense spending.
IB	Airplane pilots	X	T				X	X						X			X	X	X		X	X	X				82,000	15 to 23	Employment expected to grow as fast as average due to increased air travel. Applicants are likely to face keen competition for available jobs. Best opportunities for ex-military pilots and college graduates with flying experience.
SP	Flight attendants	X					X			X	X			X					X			X					56,000	15 to 22	Average but highly competitive.
PD	Travel agents	X					X			X	X				X				X			X					52,000	43 to 52	Employment expected to grow faster than average. Because travel expenditures often depend on business conditions, job opportunities are very sensitive to economic changes.

TYPE OF WORK AND COWORKERS	OCCUPATION	1 High School diploma	2 Technical school or apprenticeship	3 Junior college	4 College degree	5 Jobs widely scattered	6 Jobs concentrated in locations	7 Work with things	8 Work with ideas	9 Help people	10 Work with people	11 Able to see physical results of work	12 Opportunity for self-expression	13 Work as part of a team	14 Work independently	15 Work closely supervised	16 Direct activity of others	17 Generally confined to work area	18 Overtime or shift work required	19 Outdoors	20 High level of responsibility	21 Requires physical stamina	22 Work with detail	23 Repetitious work	24 Motivate others	25 Competitive	ESTIMATED EMPLOYMENT – 1980	RANGE OF POSSIBLE CHANGE IN EMPLOYMENT (HUNDREDS) 1980-1990	EMPLOYMENT PROSPECTS
MERCHANT MARINE OCCUPATIONS																													
PI	Merchant marine officers*		T		C		X		X					X			X		X		X	X					13,000	4	Little change in employment expected as size of Nation's fleet remains fairly constant. Job prospects good in offshore mineral and oil exploration.
BI	Merchant marine sailors*						X	X						X		X			X	X			X				24,000	–7	Declining as smaller crews operate new ships.
DRIVING OCCUPATIONS																													
BP	Intercity busdrivers							X			X				X				X	X							30,000	8 to 16	Below average. Keen competition for jobs.
BP	Local transit busdrivers							X			X				X				X	X							97,000	27 to 29	Average.
BD	Local truck drivers					X		X							X			X	X	X		X					1,700,000	23 to 31	Best opportunities for applicants with good driving records.
BD	Long distance truck drivers					X		X							X			X	X	X		X					575,000	23 to 31	Stiff competition is likely for available jobs in this high-paying occupation.
SCIENTIFIC AND TECHNICAL OCCUPATIONS																													
CONSERVATION OCCUPATIONS																													
BI	Foresters*				+	X		X							X		X		X	X	X	X					30,000	9 to 14	Employment expected to grow more slowly than average. Applicants are likely to face competition. Job prospects are better for persons with advanced degrees.

TYPE OF WORK AND COWORKERS	OCCUPATION	1 High School diploma	2 Technical school or apprenticeship	3 Junior college	4 College degree	5 Jobs widely scattered	6 Jobs concentrated in locations	7 Work with things	8 Work with ideas	9 Help people	10 Work with people	11 Able to see physical results of work	12 Opportunity for self-expression	13 Work as part of a team	14 Work independently	15 Work closely supervised	16 Direct activity of others	17 Generally confined to work area	18 Overtime or shift work required	19 Outdoors	20 High level of responsibility	21 Requires physical stamina	22 Work with detail	23 Repetitious work	24 Motivate others	25 Competitive	ESTIMATED EMPLOYMENT – 1980	RANGE OF POSSIBLE CHANGE IN EMPLOYMENT (HUNDREDS) 1980-1990	EMPLOYMENT PROSPECTS
SCIENTIFIC AND TECHNICAL OCCUPATIONS																													
CONSERVATION OCCUPATIONS																													
BI	Forestry technicians*			X	X		X						X					X	X		X						11,000	600	Average as use of technology in forest industry increases. Even applicants with specialized school training may face competition, however.
BI	Range managers*				+	X			X						X					X		X					4,000	26	Average as use of rangelands for grazing, recreation and wildlife habitats increases.
BI	Soil conservationists				X	X			X				X		X					X		X	X				5,000	3	Average. Prospects better in nongovernment organizations.
ENGINEERS																													
IB	Aerospace Engineers				X		X		X			X	X	X			X				X		X				68,000	43 to 52	Above average due to increased expenditures on commercial and defense programs.
IB	Agricultural Engineers				X		X		X			X	X	X			X						X				15,000	27	Above average because of increasing demand for agricultural products, modernization of farm operations, and conservation.
IB	Biomedical Engineers				X		X		X			X	X	X			X						X				4,000	27	Increased research funds could create new jobs in instrumentation and systems for delivery of health services.
IB	Ceramic Engineers				X		X		X			X	X	X			X						X				15,000	27	Above average as a result of need to develop ceramic materials for nuclear energy, electronics, defense, and medical science.

ENGINEERS

Type of Work and Coworkers	Occupation	1 High School diploma	2 Technical school or apprenticeship	3 Junior college	4 College degree	5 Jobs widely scattered	6 Jobs concentrated in locations	7 Work with things	8 Work with ideas	9 Help people	10 Work with people	11 Able to see physical results of work	12 Opportunity for self-expression	13 Work as part of a team	14 Work independently	15 Work closely supervised	16 Direct activity of others	17 Generally confined to work area	18 Overtime or shift work required	19 Outdoors	20 High level of responsibility	21 Requires physical stamina	22 Work with detail	23 Repetitious work	24 Motivate others	25 Competitive	Estimated Employment – 1980	Range of Possible Change in Employment (Hundreds) 1980-1990	Employment Prospects
IB	Chemical Engineers				X		X		X			X	X	X			X						X				55,000	23 to 32	Growing complexity and automation of chemical processes will require additional chemical engineers to design, build, and maintain plants and equipment.
IB	Civil Engineers				X		X		X			X		X			X				X		X				165,000	26 to 31	Above average as a result of growing need for housing, industrial buildings, electric power generating plants, and transportation systems. Work related to environmental pollution and energy self-sufficiency also will create openings.
IB	Electrical Engineers				X	X			X			X	X	X			X						X				325,000	35 to 47	Growing demand for computers, communications equipment, military electronics, consumer goods and power generation also should create many openings.
IB	Industrial Engineers				X	X			X				X	X			X				X		X		X		115,000	26 to 38	Better than average due to industrial growth, increasing complexity of industrial operations, expansion of automated processes, and greater emphasis on scientific management and safety engineering.
IB	Mechanical Engineers				C	X			X			X	X	X			X						X				213,000	29 to 41	Average due to growing demand for industrial machinery and machine tools. Need to develop new energy systems and to solve environmental pollution problems also will create openings.

TYPE OF WORK AND COWORKERS	OCCUPATION	1 High School diploma	2 Technical school or apprenticeship	3 Junior college	4 College degree	5 Jobs widely scattered	6 Jobs concentrated in locations	7 Work with things	8 Work with ideas	9 Help people	10 Work with people	11 Able to see physical results of work	12 Opportunity for self-expression	13 Work as part of a team	14 Work independently	15 Work closely supervised	16 Direct activity of others	17 Generally confined to work area	18 Overtime or shift work required	19 Outdoors	20 High level of responsibility	21 Requires physical stamina	22 Work with detail	23 Repetitious work	24 Motivate others	25 Competitive	ESTIMATED EMPLOYMENT – 1980	RANGE OF POSSIBLE CHANGE IN EMPLOYMENT (HUNDREDS) 1980-1990	EMPLOYMENT PROSPECTS
ENGINEERS																													
IB	Metallurgical Engineers				+		X		X			X	X	X			X						X				15,000	38 to 51	Better than average due to need to develop new metals and alloys, adapt current ones to new needs, and develop new ways to recycle solid wastes.
IB	Mining Engineers				+		X		X			X	X	X			X			X	X		X				6,000	38 to 51	Better than average due to attaining energy self-sufficiency and to developing more advanced mining systems.
ENVIRONMENTAL SCIENTISTS																													
IB	Geologists				+		X		X				X		X								X				34,000	26 to 33	Above average as domestic mineral exploration increases. Good opportunities for persons with degrees in geology.
IB	Geophysicists				+		X		X				X		X								X				12,000	26 to 33	Above average as petroleum and mining companies need additional geophysicists able to use sophisticated electronic techniques in exploration. Very good opportunities for graduates in geophysics or related areas.
IB	Meteorologists				+		X		X				X		X				X				X				4,000	8	Little change in employment expected.
IB	Oceanographers				+		X		X				X	X			X			X			X				2,800	17	Average growth is expected, competition for openings is likely. Best opportunities for persons who have Ph.D.'s; those with less education may be limited to research assistant and technician jobs.

TYPE OF WORK AND COWORKERS	OCCUPATION	1 High School diploma	2 Technical school or apprenticeship	3 Junior college	4 College degree	5 Jobs widely scattered	6 Jobs concentrated in locations	7 Work with things	8 Work with ideas	9 Help people	10 Work with people	11 Able to see physical results of work	12 Opportunity for self-expression	13 Work as part of a team	14 Work independently	15 Work closely supervised	16 Direct activity of others	17 Generally confined to work area	18 Overtime or shift work required	19 Outdoors	20 High level of responsibility	21 Requires physical stamina	22 Work with detail	23 Repetitious work	24 Motivate others	25 Competitive	ESTIMATED EMPLOYMENT – 1980	RANGE OF POSSIBLE CHANGE IN EMPLOYMENT (HUNDREDS) 1980-1990	EMPLOYMENT PROSPECTS
LIFE SCIENCE OCCUPATIONS																													
IB	Biochemists				+	X			X				X										X				16,000	20	Average due to increased funds for biochemical research and development. Favorable opportunities for advanced degree holders.
IB	Agricultural and biological scientists				+	X			X				X		X								X				125,000	17 to 20	Employment expected to grow as fast as average due to increasing expenditures for medical and agricultural research. Good opportunities for persons with advanced degrees.
IB	Soil conservationists				+	X			X				X		X								X				5,000	3	Little change in employment expected. Job prospects are better in nongovernment organizations than in government agencies.
MATHEMATICS OCCUPATIONS																													
ID	Mathematicians				+	X			X				X		X			X					X				40,000	11 to 14	Employment expected to grow more slowly than average. Favorable job prospects expected for Ph.D.'s in industry and in college faculty positions at the undergraduate level. However, competition is expected for jobs involving theoretical research. Competition for mathematician jobs likely among those without a Ph.D., although favorable job prospects are expected in related science, engineering, and computer occupations.
ID	Statisticians				+				X				X	X				X					X				26,500	17 to 25	Persons combining knowledge of statistics with a field of application, such as economics, have favorable job opportunities.

TYPE OF WORK AND COWORKERS	OCCUPATION	1 High School diploma	2 Technical school or apprenticeship	3 Junior college	4 College degree	5 Jobs widely scattered	6 Jobs concentrated in locations	7 Work with things	8 Work with ideas	9 Help people	10 Work with people	11 Able to see physical results of work	12 Opportunity for self-expression	13 Work as part of a team	14 Work independently	15 Work closely supervised	16 Direct activity of others	17 Generally confined to work area	18 Overtime or shift work required	19 Outdoors	20 High level of responsibility	21 Requires physical stamina	22 Work with detail	23 Repetitious work	24 Motivate others	25 Competitive	ESTIMATED EMPLOYMENT – 1980	RANGE OF POSSIBLE CHANGE IN EMPLOYMENT (HUNDREDS) 1980-1990	EMPLOYMENT PROSPECTS
PHYSICAL SCIENTISTS																													
IC	Astronomers				+		X		X				X		X												2,000	40	Limited with slight increases in funds for basic research. Competitive.
IC	Chemists				+	X			X				X		X												113,000	18 to 24	Employment expected to grow as fast as average as a result of increasing demand for new products, manufacturing efficiency, and energy conservation. Good opportunities are expected at all degree levels.
IC	Food technologists				+	X			X				X		X												15,000	14[2]	Employment expected to grow more slowly than average due to slow growth of the food processing industry.
IC	Physicists				+	X			X				X		X												37,000	9 to 14	Although employment will grow more slowly than average, very good jab opportunities are expected for persons with advanced degrees in physics. Persons with only a bachelor's degree will face competition for jobs as physicists, but should have favorable prospects for jobs as engineers, computer scientists, and technicians.
OTHER SCIENTIFIC AND TECHNICAL OCCUPATIONS																													
BI	Broadcast technicians	X	T			X		X						X			X		X		X		X				17,000	13 to 18	Prospects best in smaller cities. Highly competitive.

TYPE OF WORK AND COWORKERS	OCCUPATION	1 High School diploma	2 Technical school or apprenticeship	3 Junior college	4 College degree	5 Jobs widely scattered	6 Jobs concentrated in locations	7 Work with things	8 Work with ideas	9 Help people	10 Work with people	11 Able to see physical results of work	12 Opportunity for self-expression	13 Work as part of a team	14 Work independently	15 Work closely supervised	16 Direct activity of others	17 Generally confined to work area	18 Overtime or shift work required	19 Outdoors	20 High level of responsibility	21 Requires physical stamina	22 Work with detail	23 Repetitious work	24 Motivate others	25 Competitive	ESTIMATED EMPLOYMENT – 1980	RANGE OF POSSIBLE CHANGE IN EMPLOYMENT (HUNDREDS) 1980-1990	EMPLOYMENT PROSPECTS
OTHER SCIENTIFIC AND TECHNICAL OCCUPATIONS																													
BS	Drafters	X	T	X		X			X					X		X		X					X				322,000	28 to 39	Employment expected to grow faster than average due to industrial growth and increasing complexity of design problems. Best prospects for those with associate degrees or training in computer-aided drafting.
IB	Engineers	X	T	X		X		X						X		X							X				1,200,000	27 to 37	Employment expected to grow faster than average. Good employment opportunities for graduates with an engineering degree.
ID	Surveyors and surveying technicians	X	T			X			X					X			X			X			X				61,000	19 to 27	Employment expected to grow about as fast as average due to increased construction activity.
MECHANICS AND REPAIRERS																													
BI	Central office craft occupations* (telephone)	X				X		X				X			X			X	X				X	X			85,000	−6 to −7	Employment expected to show little growth and may decline as more efficient electronic switching systems replace electromechanical ones.
BI	Line installers and cable splicers*	X				X		X						X		X			X	X		X	X				70,000	5 to 19	Little change in employment is expected as technological improvements limit growth. Employment may increase, however, if modernization programs are accelerated.
BI	Telephone and PBX installers and repairers*	X				X		X						X					X	X		X	X				130,000	15 to 30	Average, due to growing demand for telephones and PBX and CENTREX systems.

TYPE OF WORK AND COWORKERS	OCCUPATION	1 High School diploma	2 Technical school or apprenticeship	3 Junior college	4 College degree	5 Jobs widely scattered	6 Jobs concentrated in locations	7 Work with things	8 Work with ideas	9 Help people	10 Work with people	11 Able to see physical results of work	12 Opportunity for self-expression	13 Work as part of a team	14 Work independently	15 Work closely supervised	16 Direct activity of others	17 Generally confined to work area	18 Overtime or shift work required	19 Outdoors	20 High level of responsibility	21 Requires physical stamina	22 Work with detail	23 Repetitious work	24 Motivate others	25 Competitive	ESTIMATED EMPLOYMENT – 1980	RANGE OF POSSIBLE CHANGE IN EMPLOYMENT (HUNDREDS) 1980-1990	EMPLOYMENT PROSPECTS
OTHER MECHANICS AND REPAIRERS																													
IB	Air-conditioning, refrigeration, and heating mechanics*					X		X				X			X				X								179,000	20 to 29	Employment expected to increase about as fast as average. Beginning mechanics may face competition for the highest paying jobs. Graduates of training programs that emphasize hands-on experience will have the best opportunities.
IB	Appliance repairers					X		X							X						X						77,000	16 to 29	Average
BI	Automobile body repairers*		A			X		X				X						X				X					150,000	23 to 37	Average
BI	Automobile mechanics*		A			X		X				X			X			X				X					845,000	24 to 33	Employment expected to increase faster than average due to growing number of automobiles. Job opportunities will be plentiful.
BD	Business machine repairers*	X	T			X		X							X								X				55,000	60 to 74	Above average as machines increase.
IB	Computer service technicians*		T			X		X							X												83,000	93 to 112	Better than average as more computer equipment is used. Very good opportunities for persons with postsecondary school training in electronics.
BI	Electric sign repairers*					X		X				X			X				X	X		X	X				16,000	(3)	Increasing.
BI	Farm equipment mechanics*		A			X		X				X			X				X	X		X					25,000	21 to 31	Best opportunities for persons familiar with farms and farm machinery.

OTHER MECHANICS AND REPAIRERS

TYPE OF WORK AND COWORKERS	OCCUPATION	1 High School diploma	2 Technical school or apprenticeship	3 Junior college	4 College degree	5 Jobs widely scattered	6 Jobs concentrated in locations	7 Work with things	8 Work with ideas	9 Help people	10 Work with people	11 Able to see physical results of work	12 Opportunity for self-expression	13 Work as part of a team	14 Work independently	15 Work closely supervised	16 Direct activity of others	17 Generally confined to work area	18 Overtime or shift work required	19 Outdoors	20 High level of responsibility	21 Requires physical stamina	22 Work with detail	23 Repetitious work	24 Motivate others	25 Competitive	ESTIMATED EMPLOYMENT – 1980	RANGE OF POSSIBLE CHANGE IN EMPLOYMENT (HUNDREDS) 1980-1990	EMPLOYMENT PROSPECTS
BI	Industrial machinery repairers*	X	A			X		X							X				X			X	X				507,000	17 to 26	Above average as more repairs will be needed to maintain growing amount of machinery used in manufacturing, coal mining, oil exploration, and other industries.
BI	Jewelers	X	A			X		X							X			X					X				28,000	16 to 27	Employment expected to grow about as fast as average as the demand for jewelry and jewelry repair increases.
BI	Piano and organ tuners and repairers	X	A				X	X							X												12,000	0	Little change expected in employment. Opportunities for trainee jobs are best for individuals with work experience or vocational training.
BI	Shoe repairs*					X		X				X			X			X				X		X			16,000	12 to 17	Employment expected to grow more slowly than average. Job prospects should be very good because of replacement needs. Because training is difficult to obtain, many openings are not filled.
BI	Television and radio service technicians*		T			X		X		X		X			X								X				83,000	31 to 43	Employment expected to grow faster than average as number of home electronic products such as television sets, video games, radios, phonographs, and tape recorders increases.
BI	Truck mechanics and bus mechanics*		A			X		X							X							X					175,000	24 to 31	Employment of truck mechanics expected to grow about as fast as average due to increasing use of trucks and buses.

TYPE OF WORK AND COWORKERS	OCCUPATION	1 High School diploma	2 Technical school or apprenticeship	3 Junior college	4 College degree	5 Jobs widely scattered	6 Jobs concentrated in locations	7 Work with things	8 Work with ideas	9 Help people	10 Work with people	11 Able to see physical results of work	12 Opportunity for self-expression	13 Work as part of a team	14 Work independently	15 Work closely supervised	16 Direct activity of others	17 Generally confined to work area	18 Overtime or shift work required	19 Outdoors	20 High level of responsibility	21 Requires physical stamina	22 Work with detail	23 Repetitious work	24 Motivate others	25 Competitive	ESTIMATED EMPLOYMENT – 1980	RANGE OF POSSIBLE CHANGE IN EMPLOYMENT (HUNDREDS) 1980-1990	EMPLOYMENT PROSPECTS
OTHER MECHANICS AND REPAIRERS																													
BI	Vending machine mechanics*						X	X				X		X	X				X			X	X				13,500	4 to 14	Below average.
BI	Watch repairers		T			X		X				X		X	X			X					X				12,000	1 to 13	Although below average, trained workers should find jobs readily available. Opportunities good for persons trained in repairing electronic watches.
HEALTH OCCUPATIONS																													
DENTAL OCCUPATIONS																													
IB	Dentists					X				X	X	X	X		X					X			X				126,000	23	Average.
SC	Dental assistants	X	T			X				X	X			X		X		X						X			140,000	38 to 42	Above average as dentists increasingly use assistants in their practice. Very good opportunities for full- and part-time jobs.
SC	Dental hygienists			X		X				X	X				X			X						X			36,000	67	Above average because of expanding population and growing awareness of importance of regular dental care.
BI	Dental laboratory technicians	X	7	7			X					X		X		X		X					X	X			53,000	29 to 49	Above average due to expansion of dental prepayment plans and increasing demand for dentures. Favorable opportunities for graduates of approved programs.

Column headings: TYPE OF WORK AND COWORKERS; OCCUPATION; High School diploma; Technical school or apprenticeship; Junior college; College degree; Jobs widely scattered; Jobs concentrated in locations; Work with things; Work with ideas; Help people; Work with people; Able to see physical results of work; Opportunity for self-expression; Work as part of a team; Work independently; Work closely supervised; Direct activity of others; Generally confined to work area; Overtime or shift work required; Outdoors; High level of responsibility; Requires physical stamina; Work with detail; Repetitious work; Motivate others; Competitive; ESTIMATED EMPLOYMENT – 1980; RANGE OF POSSIBLE CHANGE IN EMPLOYMENT (HUNDREDS) 1980-1990; EMPLOYMENT PROSPECTS

TYPE OF WORK AND COWORKERS	OCCUPATION	1	2	3	4	5	6	7	8	9	10	11	12	13	14	15	16	17	18	19	20	21	22	23	24	25	ESTIMATED EMPLOYMENT – 1980	RANGE OF POSSIBLE CHANGE IN EMPLOYMENT (HUNDREDS) 1980-1990	EMPLOYMENT PROSPECTS
MEDICAL PRACTITIONERS																													
IS	Chiropractors					+	X				X	X	X	X		X						X		X			23,000	17 to 28	New chiropractors may have difficulty establishing a practice due to dramatic increases in number of chiropractic graduates. Best opportunities in small towns and areas with few practitioners.
IS	Optometrists					+	X				X	X	X	X		X				X		X		X			27,000	21 to 31	Average.
IS	Physicians and osteopathic physicians*					+					X	X	X	X		X				X		X		X			424,000	32	Very favorable. New physicians should have little difficulty establishing new practices.
IS	Podiatrists					+	X						X	X		X						X		X			12,000	32 to 44	Opportunities for graduates to establish new practices or to enter salaried positions should be favorable.
IB	Veterinarians*					+	X						X	X		X				X	X	X		X			36,000	31 to 43	Above average because growth in number of pets and increase in veterinary research.
MEDICAL TECHNOLOGIST TECHNICIAN, AND ASSISTANT OCCUPATIONS																													
IB	Electrocardiograph technicians	X	T			X				X	X			X		X							X	X			20,000	33-39	Employment expected to grow faster than average due to use of electrocardiographs to diagnose heart diseases and to examine older patients. Best opportunities for those with postsecondary school training.

MEDICAL TECHNOLOGIST TECHNICIAN, AND ASSISTANT OCCUPATIONS

TYPE OF WORK AND COWORKERS	OCCUPATION	1 High School diploma	2 Technical school or apprenticeship	3 Junior college	4 College degree	5 Jobs widely scattered	6 Jobs concentrated in locations	7 Work with things	8 Work with ideas	9 Help people	10 Work with people	11 Able to see physical results of work	12 Opportunity for self-expression	13 Work as part of a team	14 Work independently	15 Work closely supervised	16 Direct activity of others	17 Generally confined to work area	18 Overtime or shift work required	19 Outdoors	20 High level of responsibility	21 Requires physical stamina	22 Work with detail	23 Repetitious work	24 Motivate others	25 Competitive	ESTIMATED EMPLOYMENT – 1980	RANGE OF POSSIBLE CHANGE IN EMPLOYMENT (HUNDREDS) 1980-1990	EMPLOYMENT PROSPECTS
IB	Electroen-cephalographic technologists and technicians*	X	T			X				X	X			X		X							X	X			5,000	37 to 44	Employment expected to grow faster than average due to use of EEG's in surgery and in diagnosing and monitoring patients with brain disease. Best job prospects for registered technologists and those with formal training.
IB	Medical laboratory workers*	X	2	2	2	X	X	X						X		X			X		X		X				205,000	35 to 43	Above average as physicians make wider use of laboratory facilities.
DS	Medical records technicians and clerks	X	2	2		X		X							X								X	X			55,000	46	Employment expected to grow faster than average due to increased paperwork in hospitals and other health facilities. Job prospects for graudates of approved programs will be excellent.
IB	Optometric assistants	X				X				X	X			X		X							X				18,000	33	Above average due to greater demand for eye care services. Job opportunities for persons who have completed a formal training program should be excellent.
IB	Radiologic (X-ray) technologists*				C	X		X		X				X		X			X		X		X				106,000	36 to 43	Above average as X-ray equipment is increasingly used to diagnose and treat diseases. Employment prospects generally favorable, but applicants in some areas may face competition.
SI	Respiratory therapy workers	X	2	2	2	X				X	X			X		X			X				X				50,000	52	Above average due to new applications of respiratory therapy in treating diseases.

TYPE OF WORK AND COWORKERS	OCCUPATION	1 High School diploma	2 Technical school or apprenticeship	3 Junior college	4 College degree	5 Jobs widely scattered	6 Jobs concentrated in locations	7 Work with things	8 Work with ideas	9 Help people	10 Work with people	11 Able to see physical results of work	12 Opportunity for self-expression	13 Work as part of a team	14 Work independently	15 Work closely supervised	16 Direct activity of others	17 Generally confined to work area	18 Overtime or shift work required	19 Outdoors	20 High level of responsibility	21 Requires physical stamina	22 Work with detail	23 Repetitious work	24 Motivate others	25 Competitive	ESTIMATED EMPLOYMENT – 1980	RANGE OF POSSIBLE CHANGE IN EMPLOYMENT (HUNDREDS) 1980-1990	EMPLOYMENT PROSPECTS
NURSING OCCUPATIONS																													
SC	Registered nurses*	X	4	4	4	X				X	X			X		X	X		X		X		X				1,105,000	40 to 47	Employment expected to grow faster than average. Favorable job prospects expected in rural and big city hospitals. Competition may exist in suburban hospitals and in areas with many training facilities.
SC	Licenced practical nurses*		T			X				X	X			X		X			X				X				550,000	42	Employment expected to grow faster than average as population increases and demand for health care rises. Job prospects are very good.
THERAPY AND REHABILITATION OCCUPATIONS																													
SB	Occupational therapists				X	X				X	X	X	X		X		X						X				19,000	63 to 71	Well above average due to public interest in rehabilitation of disabled persons and growth of established occupational therapy programs.
SB	Occupational therapy assistants		(2)	(2)		X				X	X	X		X		X											8,500	53	Well above average due to increased need for assistants in health care institutions. Opportunities should be very good for graduates of approved programs.
SI	Physical therapists				X	X				X	X	X	X		X		X				X		X				34,000	51 to 59	Employment expected to grow much faster than average because of increased public concern for rehabilitation services. Job prospects expected to be excellent.

TYPE OF WORK AND COWORKERS	OCCUPATION	1 High School diploma	2 Technical school or apprenticeship	3 Junior college	4 College degree	5 Jobs widely scattered	6 Jobs concentrated in locations	7 Work with things	8 Work with ideas	9 Help people	10 Work with people	11 Able to see physical results of work	12 Opportunity for self-expression	13 Work as part of a team	14 Work independently	15 Work closely supervised	16 Direct activity of others	17 Generally confined to work area	18 Overtime or shift work required	19 Outdoors	20 High level of responsibility	21 Requires physical stamina	22 Work with detail	23 Repetitious work	24 Motivate others	25 Competitive	ESTIMATED EMPLOYMENT – 1980	RANGE OF POSSIBLE CHANGE IN EMPLOYMENT (HUNDREDS) 1980-1990	EMPLOYMENT PROSPECTS
THERAPY AND REHABILITATION OCCUPATIONS																													
SB	Physical therapist assistants and aides		2	2		X				X	X	X		X		X											11,500	52	Above average due to expanding physical therapy services. Opportunities for graduates of approved programs should be excellent.
SC	Speech pathologists and audiologists				G	X				X	X	X	X		X		X				X		X				35,000	47 to 50	Employment expected to increase faster than average due to growing public concern over speech and hearing disorders. Persons with only a bachelor's degree will face keen competition for jobs.
OTHER HEALTH OCCUPATIONS																													
SI	Dietitians				+	X			X	X					X		X						X				44,000	38 to 46	Employment expected to grow faster than average in response to increasing concern for proper nutrition and food management. Favorable full- and part-time opportunities for those having a bachelor's degree in foods and nutrition or institution management and the necessary clinical experience.
PD	Health Service administrators				+	X					X				X		X		X		X		X		X		220,000	43 to 53	Well above average as quantity of patient services increases and health services management becomes more complex.
IP	Pharmacists				+	X		X		X					X				X		X		X				141,000	10 to 20	Employment expected to grow as fast as average due to aging of the population and increasing use of pharmacists in health care institutions. Employment prospects generally favorable, but keen competition is expected in some areas.

TYPE OF WORK AND COWORKERS	OCCUPATION	1 High School diploma	2 Technical school or apprenticeship	3 Junior college	4 College degree	5 Jobs widely scattered	6 Jobs concentrated in locations	7 Work with things	8 Work with ideas	9 Help people	10 Work with people	11 Able to see physical results of work	12 Opportunity for self-expression	13 Work as part of a team	14 Work independently	15 Work closely supervised	16 Direct activity of others	17 Generally confined to work area	18 Overtime or shift work required	19 Outdoors	20 High level of responsibility	21 Requires physical stamina	22 Work with detail	23 Repetitious work	24 Motivate others	25 Competitive	ESTIMATED EMPLOYMENT – 1980	RANGE OF POSSIBLE CHANGE IN EMPLOYMENT (HUNDREDS) 1980-1990	EMPLOYMENT PROSPECTS
SOCIAL SCIENTISTS																													
ID	Anthropologists				+	X			X				X		X								X				7,200	23	Most new jobs will be in nonacademic areas. Even persons with Ph.D's can expect keen competition for jobs.
ID	Economists				+	X			X				X		X								X				44,000	26 to 32	Master's and Ph.D. degree holders may face keen competition for college and university positions but can expect good opportunities in nonacademic areas. Persons with bachelor's degrees likely face keen competition.
ART, DESIGN AND COMMUNICATION OCCUPATIONS																													
PERFORMING ARTISTS																													
CB	Actors		T				X		X		X		X	X		X	X		X			X		X		X	21,000	19 to 26	Average growth. Overcrowding in this field will persist. Part-time and seasonal employment common.
CB	Dancers		T				X				X		X	X		X	X		X			X		X		X	6,500	21	Keen competition, most openings being replacements. Teaching offers the best opportunities.
CB	Musicians		T			X		X			X		X	X	X							X		X			138,000	16 to 20	Average growth, however competition will be keen.
CB	Singers		T					X			X		X	X	X							X		X			19,000	11 to 19	Employment expected to grow more slowly than average. Applicants likely to face keen competition for jobs.

DESIGN OCCUPATIONS

TYPE OF WORK AND COWORKERS	OCCUPATION	1 High School diploma	2 Technical school or apprenticeship	3 Junior college	4 College degree	5 Jobs widely scattered	6 Jobs concentrated in locations	7 Work with things	8 Work with ideas	9 Help people	10 Work with people	11 Able to see physical results of work	12 Opportunity for self-expression	13 Work as part of a team	14 Work independently	15 Work closely supervised	16 Direct activity of others	17 Generally confined to work area	18 Overtime or shift work required	19 Outdoors	20 High level of responsibility	21 Requires physical stamina	22 Work with detail	23 Repetitious work	24 Motivate others	25 Competitive	ESTIMATED EMPLOYMENT - 1980	RANGE OF POSSIBLE CHANGE IN EMPLOYMENT (HUNDREDS) 1980-1990	EMPLOYMENT PROSPECTS
CI	Architects				X	X		X				X				X		X						X			79,500	33 to 41	Employment expected to rise faster than average, but competition for jobs likely.
CB	Commercial and graphic artists and designers		T	X		X		X				X				X		X						X			120,000	2 to 11	Keen competition expected to continue in field. Those with above average talent and skills will be in demand.
BC	Retail display workers	X					X	X				X		X		X						X		X			26,000	19 to 27	Employment expected to grow as fast as average because of the populatiry of visual merchandising—the use of merchandise to decorate stores. Best prospects for those with artistic talent and some college background.
CB	Floral designers	X				X		X				X	X			X		X					X	X			56,000	10	Employment will grow more slowly than average as floral outlets in supermarkets increase and people buy moore loose flowers rather than arrangements.
Ci	Industrial designers		X		X			X	X			X	X														13,000	10	Below average as trend away from frequent redesign of household products, automobiles, and industrial equipment continues.
CI	Interior designers		X		X				X		X	X	X		X				X				X			X	35,000	25	Increasing use of design services in business and homes should cause average growth. Competition for jobs likely. Best opportunities for talented college graduates in interior design and graduates of professional interior design schools.

TYPE OF WORK AND COWORKERS	OCCUPATION	1 High School diploma	2 Technical school or apprenticeship	3 Junior college	4 College degree	5 Jobs widely scattered	6 Jobs concentrated in locations	7 Work with things	8 Work with ideas	9 Help people	10 Work with people	11 Able to see physical results of work	12 Opportunity for self-expression	13 Work as part of a team	14 Work independently	15 Work closely supervised	16 Direct activity of others	17 Generally confined to work area	18 Overtime or shift work required	19 Outdoors	20 High level of responsibility	21 Requires physical stamina	22 Work with detail	23 Repetitious work	24 Motivate others	25 Competitive	ESTIMATED EMPLOYMENT - 1980	RANGE OF POSSIBLE CHANGE IN EMPLOYMENT (HUNDREDS) 1980-1990	EMPLOYMENT PROSPECTS
DESIGN OCCUPATIONS																													
CI	Landscape architects				X	X			X			X	X										X				15,000	33	Employment expected to grow faster than average due to increases in new construction and city and regional environmental planning. Best job prospects for those with graduate degrees in landscape architecture.
CB	Photographers		7	7	X		X				X	X		X										X			91,000	14 to 24	Employment expected to grow about as fast as average. Portrait and commercial photographers likely to face keen competition. Good opportunities in areas such as law enforcement and scientific and medical research photography.
COMMUNICATIONS RELATED OCCUPATIONS																													
CI	Reporters and correspondents				X	X			X			X	X		X						X						57,000	22 to 32	Employment expected to grow about as fast as average. Best opportunities on newspapers and magazines in small towns and suburbs and for graduates who have specialized in news-editorial studies and completed an internship.
CI	Radio and television announcers and newscasters	X				X			X				X	X				X				X					51,000	28 to 34	Employment expected to increase faster than average as new stations are licensed and as cable television stations do more of their own programming. Keen competition likely for openings, however. Best prospects in small cities.

TYPE OF WORK AND COWORKERS	OCCUPATION	1 High School diploma	2 Technical school or apprenticeship	3 Junior college	4 College degree	5 Jobs widely scattered	6 Jobs concentrated in locations	7 Work with things	8 Work with ideas	9 Help people	10 Work with people	11 Able to see physical results of work	12 Opportunity for self-expression	13 Work as part of a team	14 Work independently	15 Work closely supervised	16 Direct activity of others	17 Generally confined to work area	18 Overtime or shift work required	19 Outdoors	20 High level of responsibility	21 Requires physical stamina	22 Work with detail	23 Repetitious work	24 Motivate others	25 Competitive	ESTIMATED EMPLOYMENT - 1980	RANGE OF POSSIBLE CHANGE IN EMPLOYMENT (HUNDREDS) 1980-1990	EMPLOYMENT PROSPECTS
COMMUNICATIONS RELATED OCCUPATIONS																													
IC	Technical writers					X			X				X	X				X					X				25,000	26 to 36	Better than average growth. Best opportunities for people with both writing ability and a scientific or technical background.
ID	Geographers				+	X		X	X			X		X	X								X				15,000	25	Average. Best prospects for advance degree holders in the nonacademic market.
ID	Historians				X	X			X						X								X				20,000	– 9	Employment expected to decline. Keen competition is anticipated, particularly for academic positions. Best opportunities for Ph.D.'s with a strong background in quantitative research methods.
ID	Political scientists				X	X			X														X				15,000	14	Employment expected to increase more slowly than average. Keen competition likely, especially for academic positions. Best opportunities for advanced degree holders with training in applied fields such as public administration or public policy.
IS	Psychologists				X	X			X	X	X										X				X		106,000	22 to 27	Employment expected to grow as fast as average. Graduates face increasing competition, particularly for academic positions. Best prospects for doctoral degree holders trained in applied areas, such as clinical, counseling, health, and industrial psychology.
IS	Sociologists				X	X				X		X											X				21,000	6 to 8	Below average growth. Best opportunities for Ph.D.'s trained in statistical research. very competitive below Ph.D. level.

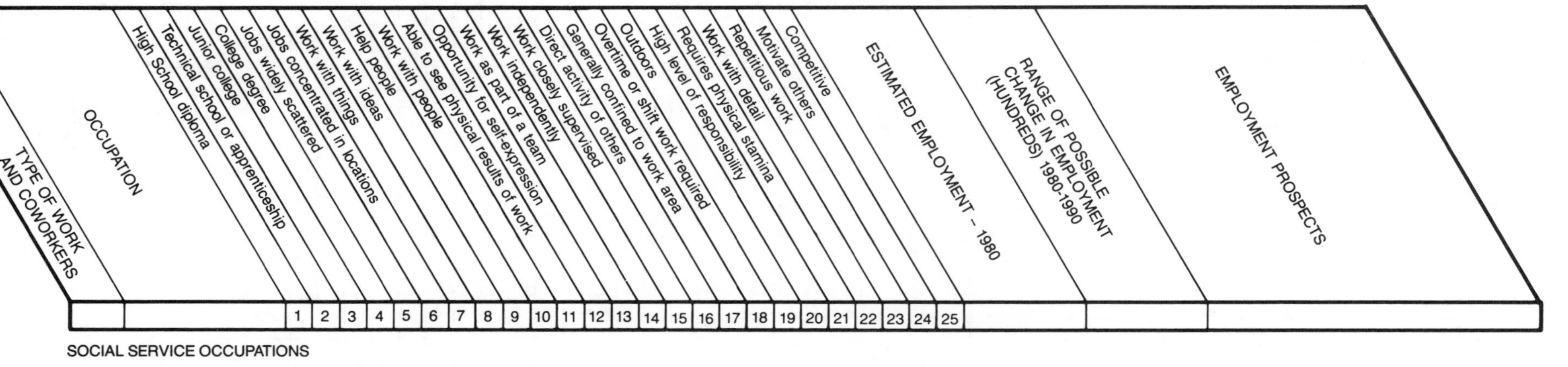

SOCIAL SERVICE OCCUPATIONS

COUNSELING

TYPE OF WORK AND COWORKERS	OCCUPATION	1 High School diploma	2 Technical school or apprenticeship	3 Junior college	4 College degree	5 Jobs widely scattered	6 Jobs concentrated in locations	7 Work with things	8 Work with ideas	9 Help people	10 Work with people	11 Able to see physical results of work	12 Opportunity for self-expression	13 Work as part of a team	14 Work independently	15 Work closely supervised	16 Direct activity of others	17 Generally confined to work area	18 Overtime or shift work required	19 Outdoors	20 High level of responsibility	21 Requires physical stamina	22 Work with detail	23 Repetitious work	24 Motivate others	25 Competitive	ESTIMATED EMPLOYMENT – 1980	RANGE OF POSSIBLE CHANGE IN EMPLOYMENT (HUNDREDS) 1980-1990	EMPLOYMENT PROSPECTS
SI	School counselors				+	X				X				X							X				X		53,000	0	Little change expected in employment due to sharply declining enrollments in secondary schools.
SD	Employment counselors				+	X				X											X						6,400	(3)	Dependent on public funding. Keen competition.
SI	Rehabilitation counselors				+	X				X											X						25,000	(3)	Employment growth depends upon government funding for vocational rehabilitation agencies. Some openings are expected with insurance companies and consulting firms.
SI	Clergy				+	X				X							X				X				X		253,000	(3)	Protestant ministers face competition because of mergers. Reform rabbis and Orthodox clergy will also face competition. Catholic priests declining.

Footnotes

1. Educational requirements vary by industry or employer.
2. Educational requirements vary according to type of work.
3. Estimate not available.
4. Diploma, baccalaureate, and associate degree programs prepare R.N. candidates for licensure.
5. Teachers only.
6. Decrease in employment is expected to be greater than number of openings.
7. Training programs are available from vocational schools or junior colleges.
8. Range less than one percent.

T Specialized or technical training needed.

\+ Educational requirements beyond a bachelor's degree.

A Availability of official apprenticeship programs.

* Workers use dangerous equipment or material or work in dangerous surroundings.

** B = Body Workers; D, Data Detail; P, Persuaders; S, Service Workers; C, Creative Artists; I, Investigators.

PART II: DEVELOPING A GAME PLAN

1. Your Educational Alternatives

Here are 13 of the most common choices of things to do next made by high school students. Rank them, by numbering them 1 to 13 in their order of attractiveness to you.

______ Community college, either 2-year technical training or a program offering transfer to a four-year college

______ Four-year college or university

______ Full-time work

______ Military service

______ Business or technical school

______ Part-time work/part-time college

______ Apprenticeship program

______ Volunteer organization (usually social or religious service)

______ Unemployment/postponing any commitment

______ Marriage/homemaking career

______ Self-employment/start your own business

______ Fail to graduate and stay in high school

______ Stopping off (taking a year off between high school and college or other commitment)

Now brainstorm other options you have about your future. The objective of brainstorming is to generate as many ideas about your future as you can. If possible, recruit a friend to help brainstorm about your future.

Groundrules of Brainstorming

1. Make your list of possibilities as long as possible.
2. Put everything in writing.
3. Allow no rights, wrongs, evaluations, or examinations.
4. Allow for bizarre and irrational as well as usual and predictable choices.
5. Do not question, discuss, or defend any possibility.

	Acceptable	Unacceptable
I could...		
I could...		
I could...		
I could...		
I could...		
I could...		
I could...		
I could...		
I could...		
I could...		

When you have generated as many ideas as possible, determine whether you like or dislike the idea. Indicate this with a check in the appropriate column.

2. Possible Training Programs and College Majors

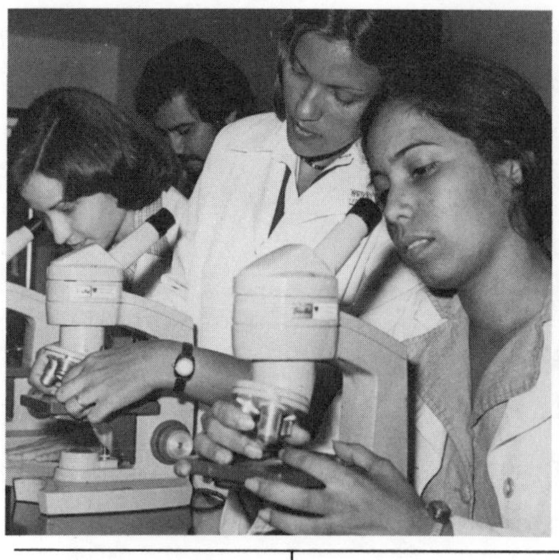

Every worker should consider it necessary to receive edu cation beyond high school. In the future, there will be fewer opportunities in unskilled occupations. U.S. census statistics continue to show a relationship between the amount of training after high school and the amount of training after high school and the amount of money earned.

A two-year program in a community college can provide you with training that offers more employment security, a decent income, and a growing future. Two-year training programs are today's bargain in higher education for many.

In the next decade, three out of every four jobs will require a one- or two-year specialized certificate or associate degree. Today's employers are anxious to hire skilled, trained workers who have recent, relevant training in their fields.

The Body Workers

These are samples of courses that prepare workers for physically active and technical jobs, work involving tools or machines; the jobs may be in the skilled trades, technical, service, or professional trades.

College Programs
Agricultural Engineering
Botany
Food Service
Forestry
Horticulture
Landscape Architecture
Occupational Therapy

Vocational Schools
Agricultural Power Equipment
Air Conditioning Technology
Aircraft Assembly
Aircraft Field Services
Airline Communications
Appliance Servicing
Automobile Mechanics
Aviation Electronics
Baking
Bartending
Body and Fender Repair
Building Construction
Business Machine Servicing
Cargo Supervision
Carpentry
Computer Technology
Dairy Technology
Dental Lab Technology
Diesel Mechanics and Technology
Dispatcher
Drafting
Dressmaking
Dry Cleaning
Earth Moving Machinery
Electrical Power Technology
Electroplating
Engraving
Fisheries
Flight Training
Floor Covering
Floristry
Forestry Technology
Heating Technology
Horticulture
Landscape Architecture
Laundering
Livestock Procurement
Locksmithing
Marine Engineering
Masonry
Metal Trades
Microwave Technology
Motorcycle Repair
Moving
Navigation Technology
Nursery Management
Painting
Paperhanging
Park and Recreation Work
Photography
Pilot
Plastering
Plumbing
Polygraph Technology
Power Plant Mechanics
Printing Technology
Radar Technology
Radio, TV Repair
Restaurant Practice
Refrigeration
Sewing Machine Operation
Ship Building
Sound Systems Technology
Tailoring
Tiling
Tractor Mechanics
Typesetting
Upholstery
Veterinary Technology
Watchmaking
Water Treatment
Welding
Wildlife Management

Military Training Programs
Air Traffic Control
Asphalt Equipment Operation
Audio Specialist
Aviation Electronics
Aviation Machinery
Boilermaking
Bricklaying
Butchering
Carpentry
Commissary
Cooking
Crane Operation
Crawler Tractor Operation
Cryptography
Disbursing Clerk
Dispatching
Driving
Electronics
Electronics Technician
Equipment Repair
Fire Fighting

Grader Operation
Heating and Cooling Technology
Lithographer
Maintenance Administration
Masonry
Painting
Pipe Fitting
Platemaking
Plumbing
Presswork
Radar
Radio Operation
Sheet Metal Work
Shoe Repair
Silk-screen Printing
Storekeeper
Structural Mechanics
Telephone Operation
Textile and Leather Repair
Welding
Woodworking

Apprenticeships
Aircraft Fabrication
Airplane Mechanics
Arborist
Asbestos Work
Auto Mechanics
Boilermaking
Bookbinding
Stationary Engineering
Steam Fitting
Stonemasonry
Textile Technology
Tile Laying
Tool and Die Making
Truck Mechanics
Upholstery
Wood Carving

Cooperative Programs
Aerospace Technology
Brewer
Bricklaying
Butchery
Cabinetmaking
Candymaking
Canvas Worker
Carpentry
Carpet Laying
Cement Masonry
Composition
Cosmetology
Dental Technology
Electrical Technology
Engraving
Ironwork
Jewelry
Lathe Making
Leatherwork
Lithography
Meat Cutting
Molding
Ophthalmic Technology
Painting
Patternmaking
Photoengraving
Pipefitting
Plastering
Platemaking
Plumbing
Presswork
Rigging
Roofing
Sheet Metal Work

Agriculture
Applied Mechanics
Aviation Maintenance
Building Construction
Carpentry
Ceramics
Chemical Technology
Electronics
Fire Protection
Forestry
Recreation Technology
Welding

The Data Detail

The following courses prepare workers for white-collar jobs involving clerical or numerical tasks.

College Majors
Accounting
Actuarial Science
Appraisal
Business
Business Administration
Business Teacher Education
Computer Programming
Finance
International Business
Real Estate and Urban Land Economics

Vocational Programs
Accountancy
Banking
Bookkeeping
Checker, Cashier
Claims Adjuster
Computer Operation
Computer Programming
Court Reporting

Data Processing
Estimating
Insurance Adjusting
Keypunch
PBX Switchboard
Tax Preparation
Typing
Word Processing

Cooperative Programs
Accounting
Administration
Aviation Administration
Data Processing
Medical Technology
Secretarial Science
Secretary
Stenography

Military Training
Bookkeeping
Computer Operator
Court Reporter
Journalism
Legal Services Assistant
Machine Accounting Clerk
Medical Records Clerk
Personnel
Programmer
Stenographer

The Persuaders

These college majors and vocational programs prepare workers to hold jobs where they persuade people to perform some kind of action.

College Majors
Communication Arts
Educational Administration
Health Services Administration
Industrial Relations
International Relations
Law
Management
Political Science
Programming
Public Administration
Retailing
Urban and Regional Planning

Vocational Schools
Advertising
Airline Reservations
Apartment House Management
Auctioneering
Buying
Credit and Collection
Fashion Merchandising
Food Service
Hotel and Motel Management
Insurance Sales
Market Training
Medical Office Management
Merchandising
Real Estate Sales
Receptionish
Retail Management
Travel Agent
Travel Guide

Cooperative Programs
Advertising
Fashion Merchandising
Marketing
Retail Management
Sales Training

The Service Workers

The following courses prepare workers to hold jobs where they heal, teach, or help people.

College Majors
Behavioral Science
Child Development
Communication Disorders
Counseling
Education
Nursing
Occupational Therapy
Physical Therapy
Psychology
Social Studies
Social Work
Sociology

Vocational Schools
Child Care and Guidance
Community Organization
Cosmetology
Dental Assistance
Dietetics
Electrical Technology
Family Assistance
Flight Attendant

Hospital Admitting Clerk
Infant Care
Inhalation Therapy
Law Enforcement
Medical Assistance
Medical Records Technician
Nurse's Aide
Optical Dispensing
Paramedic Training
Practical Nursing
Radiation Therapy

Military
Dental Technician Specialist
E.K.G., E.E.G. Specialist
Operating Room Assistant
Physical Therapy Technologist
Prosthetic Appliance Specialist
Psychiatric Technician
Radiation Therapy Technologist
Social Work Assistant
X-ray Operator

The Creative Artists

These courses prepare workers to use words, music, graphics, dance, painting or other forms of art, to express thought or feeling in a creative way.

College Majors
Art
Broadcasting
Classics
Communication Arts
Comparative Literature
Dance
English
Interior Design
Journalism
Languages
Music
Photography
Theater and Drama
TV Production

Vocational Programs
Acting
Advertising Art
Architecture
Bookbinding
Broadcasting
Cartography
Cartooning
Ceramics
Costume
Creative Writing
Dance
Darkroom Techniques
Drafting
Educational Media Technology
Engraving
Fashion Design
Fashion Illustration
Furniture Design
Interior Design
Journalism
Layout
Package Design

Pantomime
Photography
Playwriting
Radio Announcing
Refrigeration Technology
Sculpture
Sign Painting

Silk-screen Printing
Technical Illustrating
Theater Production
TV Production
Weaving

Military Programs
Communications
Illustrating
Photography
Special Services

The Investigators

These courses prepare workers to investigate how the world is put together. The work usually involves scientific or laboratory work.

College Majors
Anatomy
Anthropology
Astronomy
Bacteriology
Behavioral Disabilities
Behavioral Science
Biochemistry
Biology
Biomedical Engineering
Biophysics
Chemical Engineering
Chemistry
Dietetics
Earth Science
Electrical Engineering
Endocrinology
Entomology
Forestry
Genetics
Geography
History
Horticulture
Industrial Engineering
Medical Science
Meteorology
Neurophysiology
Neurosciences
Oceanography
Pathology
Pharmacy
Physical Therapy
Physiology
Plant Genetics
Poultry Science
Quantitative Analysis
Statistics
Zoology

Vocational Schools and/or Technical Institutes
Aerospace Engineering
Architectural Engineering
Ceramics
Chemical
Civil Engineering
Industrial Engineering Technology
Metallurgical Engineering
Mechanical Engineering
Mineral Engineering
Oceanographic Engineering
Petroleum Engineering
Plastics Engineering
Quality Control
Surveying
Technical Writing
Testing Techology

Military Training
Intelligence Specialist
Radar Technologist
Sonar Specialist
Structural Engineering
Technical Engineering
Weather Observer

3. Choosing a College

Fill in the next few pages if you are seriously considering going to college either right after graduation or at some later date. If you think you *might* consider going to college someday, it's useful to fill them in, too.

The following list includes some of the reasons for choosing a particular college. Rank the five that you feel are the reasons which most influence you. Give a *1* to your strongest reason, a *2* to the next strongest, and so on. Be sure to read all the reasons listed here, and also consider any others you can think of that influence you or your friends in the choice before you.

______ Go to the college nearest home.

______ Go to a college where you know other students.

______ Go to a college recruiting hardest for students.

______ Go to the college with most desired program.

______ Make a systematic survey of the universities and colleges available and select the one most meaningful to you.

_______ Choose the college according to its tuition and living fees.

_______ Go to the college whose admission requirements can be met.

_______ Go to the college you believe will best affect your selection of friends, spouse, religious, political, and career values.

_______ Go to the college which will best qualify you for graduate school.

_______ Go to the college with the most collegiate, social atmosphere.

_______ Go to the college with an intellectual atmosphere, giving much academic responsibility to students.

_______ Go to the college that is parent's choice.

_______ Other (explain)____.

Check the appropriate answer to these questions.

	Yes	*No*
Are you willing to commit yourself to a lengthy, expensive education?		
Do you want to enlarge your intellectual horizons?		
Do you want to develop skills for a specific occupation demanding college?		
Do you want to meet people with similar interests?		
Do you want to learn how to learn and how to think clearly?		
Are you willing to give hours each day to study and practice?		

You should probably have three or more "yes" answers if you are ready to benefit from college and make it worth the investment.

Should you choose a large school or a small school?

Check which of these items is true of your behavior.

- ______ Tend to cut class.
- ______ Frequently tend to quit what you are doing.
- ______ Shun active participation in class and school activities
- ______ Tend to get lost in crowds.
- ______ Need encouragement to be involved and productive in many activities.
- ______ Shy, tend to socialize with only a few people.
- ______ Friendly, frequently greet people and mix well with people.

- ______ Will attend class without supervision or the teacher knowing you are there.
- ______ Persevere in the path which you choose.
- ______ Have a history of active participation in class and school functions.
- ______ Have assumed responsibility and importance in a wide range of school activities.
- ______ Have a history of very productive school activity.
- ______ Would utilize extensive facilities, well-stocked library, etc.

If most of your checks are in the left column, a small school may be best for you. If most of your checks are on the right then a large school may be best.

An important part of deciding on a college is coming to terms with expenses involved. You will need to know specific costs for tuition, extra fees, room and board, books, how much it will cost you to get back and forth from school, what your personal expenses will be.

You should compare the costs at each of the schools you have considered attending, and weigh these factors with the others when you are choosing the college you will attend.

The best resource for information about scholarships and financial aid is published each year and available free. It is *Meeting Your College Costs* and can be ordered from The College Entrance Examination Board, Box 592, Princeton, NJ 08540. It gives step-by-step directions for when and where to apply for financial aid.

Other factors to consider when choosing a college

1. Two-year or four-year?
   Do you have a poor high school record? Most two-year community colleges have open admissions policies and programs to develop academic skills. Are finances a concern? Again, a community college may be the solution since for two years you may live at home, attend school for a low tuition, and then complete your training at a more expensive four-year university.

2. Academic difficulty
   Arriving at a college which will be sufficiently stimulating for you should involve evaluating your college board scores and comparing them with your high school grades. The *College Handbook* edited by Douglas D. Dillenbeck and the *Comparative Guide To American Colleges* by Max Birnbaum and James Cass are especially helpful in matching your abilities with the right school.

3. Location
   Do you want to be in the heart of a large city or do you do best in a small-town atmosphere?

Which college major is best?

In a recent survey, college graduates were asked which college courses they found most useful in their work. The vast majority of graduates surveyed said their education increased their general knowledge and helped them get a good job. But less than one quarter said their training was useful for increasing their leadership abilities or in helping them select career goals.

When asked which courses they would recommend to college students, the graduates most frequently suggested courses in business administration, English, and psychology. Other highly recommended courses were economics, accounting, and mathematics. Regardless of their occupations, graduates stressed the need for skills in communication—writing and speaking—administration, and working with people.

You may wish to select a major immediately upon entering college. If so, you probably already have an idea of your major interest. Whether or not you have already made up your mind about your major, you should discuss it with people who are already in the field that interests you, with your high school guidance counselor, and the admissions and major department counselors at the college. This can be done by correspondence and/or in person. Your friends and family may provide insight, too, in career areas they know, and in helping you to analyze your own special talents and problem areas. If family sessions about your choice become too emotional, it sometimes is a great help to have a third, outside party present, like the high school career counselor, or a teacher or family friend who knows something about the field.

Colleges usually allow a year or two of attendance before requiring the selection of a major. If you do not already know what you want your major to be, you will have time to think about it while you learn more about more areas of concentration. The broad curriculum that is usually required in the freshman year is an aid to your decision making for that reason.

Should you join the military?

Military service provides an alternative to many high school graduates, and also, may provide a vehicle for later education. Think over the questions listed below, for clues to whether or not you would be happy in the military. Write in yes or no.

_______ Do you want to explore life before deciding on long-range plans?

_______ Do you want to learn a lifelong technical skill or even a college degree with no financial commitment?

_______ Do you want to live away from home and meet many new people?

_______ Do you want to begin a career right away that can lead to a early, well-paying retirement?

_______ Do you want adequate salary immediately plus housing, meals, 30 day vacation, and PX privileges?

_______ Do you want to travel?

_______ Do you want to be eligible for veteran's benefits like education, counseling, preferred morgage rates, life insurance?

_______ Can you accept that in the event of war you will risk physical injury?

_______ Can you live a regimented life style with a set time to get up, eat and go to bed?

_______ Can you accept very authoritarian leadership where an order is an order?

_______ Can you live in barracks with almost no privacy?

_______ Can you live in a situation where it is almost impossible to resign, as you can in private employment?

_______ Would it be good to put yourself in a situation where you will be forced to stay with the job long enough to learn its rewards and successes?

If you answer "yes" to most of these questions, military service may provide a good alternative for you. You may want to talk to friends who have enlisted, as well as representatives of the military services in your area.

4. Choosing a Vocational School

Vocational schools provide hands-on training with actual equipment used in such fields as beauty culture, auto mechanics, computer technology. Vocational schools usually provide job placement services as well.

About 40 percent of each day in the vocational school is spent in job-like situations; the rest is spent in classes. Vocational schools are achievement-oriented; they contract with you to teach you the minimum skills you will need to get a job in a given field.

The following questions will help you decide whether vocational school is right for you:

______ Would you like to learn things that help you do something concrete and productive on your job?

______ Do you want to complete your training in a relatively short period of time?

Consumer's Guide to Vocational Schools

The following are some questions that should be thought over when shopping for the best vocational school. Find out the answers and consider them carefully.

What are my objectives?

How do students at the school rate their courses?

Who are the teachers? (Teachers at private schools often have more practical experience than teachers at community college vocational programs.)

Do I have the necessary prerequisites? (If you are deficient in high school math, science, or some other requirement, find out how you can fulfill that requirement.)

Ask yourself, "What will happen to me if I enroll in this school?"

What kinds of students will be in class with you?

What would be the total cost to complete the training? (Include expenses as well as tuition.)

What proportion of students complete their training at this institution?

How much money do graduates make on their jobs after training?

How do employers who have hired graduates of the school evaluate the school?

Is the school listed with the Better Business Bureau, the State Department of Public Instruction, or an accrediting agency? (If the school is not accredited, be very careful in evaluating it.)

Factors to Look for When Studying a Vocational School Catalog

Will placement assistance, housing assistance, or parking cost extra? (Placement services should be provided without additional charge.)

Are the endorsements and testimonials for the school current, relevant and truthful?

Do its publicity photos and illustrations create false impressions?

Does the equipment in the photographs actually belong to the school?

Does the catalog have a recent date?

Sources for Finding Vocational Schools

Yellow Pages under "Schools"

Consumer Advice Office of your state. It publishes a *Directory of Approved Private Trade and Technical Schools.*

5. Consider an Apprenticeship

Apprenticeship is a training system, based on written agreement, by which a worker learns a skilled craft or trade. Apprenticeship programs are conducted by the voluntary cooperation of labor unions, management, schools, and government. They are usually conducted wholly on the job.

An apprenticeship program may be right for you if you can answer "yes" to most of the following questions.

Do you enjoy working with your hands and are you good at it?

Are you patient enough to work with precision?

Do you definitely want to learn a skilled trade that is taught through an apprenticeship?

Are you willing to invest the next two to five years learning a trade?

Can you afford to live on a low wage scale while learning?

Do you value the security and regular salary increases that go with the trade after you complete an apprenticeship?

Are you willing to settle down, make a choice, and be committed to it?

Are you between 18 and 30 years of age and in good physical health?

Can you pass the entrance test? (State employment services or apprenticeship information Centers, ALF-CIO, The Urban League, and Worker's Defense League, among others, have programs that prepare people for the entrance exams.)

For information about apprenticeships, write to:

U.S. Department of Apprenticeship and Training
Department of Labor
Washington, DC 20202.

More information about opportunities in your area is available from the nearest regional office. These offices, along with the states they serve are as follows:

Region I
(CT, ME, MA, NH, RI, VT)
Room 1703-A
John Kennedy Federal Bldg.
Government Center
Boston, MA 02203

Region II
(NY, NJ, Puerto Rico, Virgin Islands)
Room 906, Parcel Post Bldg.
341 Ninth Ave.
New York, NY 10001

Region III
(DE, MD, PA, VA, WV)
P.O. Box 8796
Philadelphia, PA 19101

Region IV
(AL, FL, GA, KY, MS, NC, SC, TN)
Room 729
1317 Peachtree St., N.W.
Atlanta, GA 30309

Region V
(IL, IN, MI, MN, OH, WI)
219 S. Dearborn St.
Chicago, IL 60604

Region VI
(AR, LA, NM, OK, TX)
Room 312, Mayflower Building
411 N. Akard St.
Dallas, TX 75201

Region VII
(IA, KS, MO, NE)
Room 2107, Federal Office Bldg.
911 Walnut St.
Kansas City, MO 64106

Region VIII
(CO, MT, ND, SD, UT, WY)
Room 314, New Custom House
19th and Stout Sts.
Denver, CO 80202

Region IX
(AZ, CA, HI, NV, Trust Territories)
Room 10451, Federal Building
450 Golden Gate Ave.
San Francisco, CA 94102

Region X
(AK, ID, WA, OR)
Room 1809, Smith Tower
506 Second Ave.
Seattle, WA 98104

Arizona
Arizona Apprenticeship Council
1623-B West Adams
Phoenix, AZ 85007

California
Div. of Apprenticeship Standards
Dept. of Industrial Relations
455 Golden Gate Ave.
P.O. Box 603
San Francisco, CA 94102

Colorado
Apprenticeship Council
Industrial Commission Offices
200 E. 9th Ave., Rm. 216
Denver, CO 80203

Connecticut
Apprenticeship Training Div.
Labor Dept.
200 Folly Brook Blvd.
Wethersfield, 06109

Delaware
State Apprenticeship and Training Council
Dept. of Labor and Industry
618 N. Union St.
Wilmington, 19805

District of Columbia
D.C. Apprenticeship Council
555 Pennsylvania Ave., NW, Rm. 307
Washington, DC, 20212

Florida
Bureau of Apprenticeship
Div. of Labor
State of Florida Dept. of Commerce
Caldwell Building
Tallahassee, 32304

Hawaii
Apprenticeship Div.
Dept. of Labor and Industrial Relations
825 Mililani St.
Honolulu, 96813

Kansas
Apprenticeship Training Div.
Dept. of Labor
401 Topeka Blvd.
Topeka, 66603

Kentucky
Kentucky State Apprenticeship Council
Dept. of Labor
Frankfort, 40601

Louisiana
Div. of Apprenticeship
Dept. of Labor
State Capital Annex
P.O. Box 44063
Baton Rouge, 70804

Maine
Maine Apprenticeship Council
Dept. of Labor and Industry
State Office Building
Augusta, 04330

Maryland
Maryland Apprenticeship and Training Council
Dept. of Labor and Industry
203 E. Baltimore St.
Baltimore, 21202

Massachusetts
Div. of Apprentice Training
Dept. of Labor and Industry
State Office Building
Government Center
100 Cambridge St.
Boston, 02202

Minnesota
Div. of Voluntary Apprenticeship
Dept. of Labor and Industry
110 State Office Building
St.Paul, 55110

Montana
Montana Apprenticeship Council
1331 Helena Ave.
Helena, 59601

Nevada
Nevada Apprenticeship Council
Dept. of Labor
Capitol Building
Carson City, 89701

New Hampshire
New Hampshire Apprenticeship Council
Dept. of Labor
State House Annex
Concord, 03301

New Mexico
New Mexico Apprenticeship Council
Labor and Industrial Commission
1010 National Building
505 Marquette, NW
Albuquerque, 87101

New York
Bureau of Apprenticeship Training
Dept. of Labor
The Campus, Building #12
Albany, 12226

North Carolina
Div. of Apprenticeship Training
Dept. of Labor
Raleigh, 27603

Ohio
Ohio State Apprenticeship Training
Department of Industrial Relations
220 Parsons Ave., Rm. 314
Columbus, 43215

Oregon
Apprenticeship and Training Div.
Oregon Bureau of Labor
Rm. 115, Labor and Industries Building
Salem, 97310

Pennsylvania
Pennsylvania Apprenticeship and Training Council
Dept. of Labor and Industry
Rm. 1547, Labor and Industry Building
Harrison, 17120

Puerto Rico
Apprenticeship Div. Dept. of Labor
414 Barbosa Ave.
Hato Rey, 00917

Rhode Island
Rhode Island Apprenticeship Council
Dept. of Labor
235 Promenade St.
Providence, 02908

Utah
Utah State Apprenticeship Council
Industrial Commission
431 S. 6th St., Rm. 225
Salt Lake City, 84102

Vermont
Vermont Apprenticeship Council
Dept. of Industrial Relations
State Office Building.
Montpelier, 05602

Virginia
Div. of Apprenticeship Training
Dept. of Labor and Industry
P.O. Box 1814
9th St. Office Building
Richmond, 23214

Virgin Islands
Div. of Apprenticeship and Training
Dept. of Labor
Christiansted, St. Croix, 00820

Washington
Apprenticeship Div.
Dept. of Labor and Industries
314 E. 4th Ave.
Olympia, 98594

Wisconsin
Div. of Apprenticeship and Training
Dept. of Labor, Industry, and Human Relations
Box 2209
Madison, 53701

6. Consider Correspondence Schools, Cooperative Programs, and On-the-job Training

CORRESPONDENCE SCHOOLS

Correspondence schools offer courses which can be completed at home. You receive textbooks, study guides, assignments, and tests through the mail. Some schools use cassette tapes as well. You complete an assignment on your own and mail it to the school, where it is graded and returned. A correspondence school may be right for you if you answer "yes" to most of these questions:

_______ Are you self-disciplined enough to adhere to a study schedule which is entirely voluntary?

_______ Are you a good finisher as well as beginner? (Many people begin correspondence courses, but few complete them.)

_______ Are you good at working alone, proceeding at your own pace?

_______ Are you highly motivated and self-disciplined?

_______ Must you work while you complete your education?

_______ Do you live where classroom courses are unavailable?

The National Home Study Council is the recognized accrediting agency for correspondence schools. Beware of any school not accredited by the council, since there have been a few instances of correspondence schools failing to live up to acceptable standards in business and educational practices.

Some colleges and universities offer courses by correspondence. Usually the student can do the studying and writing by correspondence, and the college gives a final exam at the college or a branch. Sometimes, however, it's possible to set up a procedure for final exams in your own community if you are a great distance from the school.

Correspondence courses in combination with television classes on regular commercial or educational television channels are another convenient alternative. They may save you time and money, and may also provide opportunities for review or monitoring of a course just as a viewer.

COOPERATIVE PROGRAMS

Cooperative programs are programs in which the student attends classes part of the time and works at a related job part-time. There are cooperative programs leading to bachelor's degrees as well as cooperative vocational programs. What you study in the classroom is the kind of work you do on your job.

A cooperative program may be best for you if you are willing to devote a period of time to part-time work, and part-time learning.

For a complete list of programs and schools that offer cooperative programs, consult the *Directory of Cooperative Education,* found in the reference section of most libraries.

ON-THE-JOB TRAINING PROGRAMS

Many people choose to go to work full time, directly from high school. There are many on-the-job training programs in which these people can get training.

Do you want to complete your training in a relatively short period of time? (a week to a few months?) Do you want to earn full pay while you learn? Are you interested in working for a giant corporation like IBM, Sperry Rand, AT&T, or a city hospital or police or fire department? All of these are employers with training programs for many positions. Many other concerns have training programs as well.

7. Predict the Results

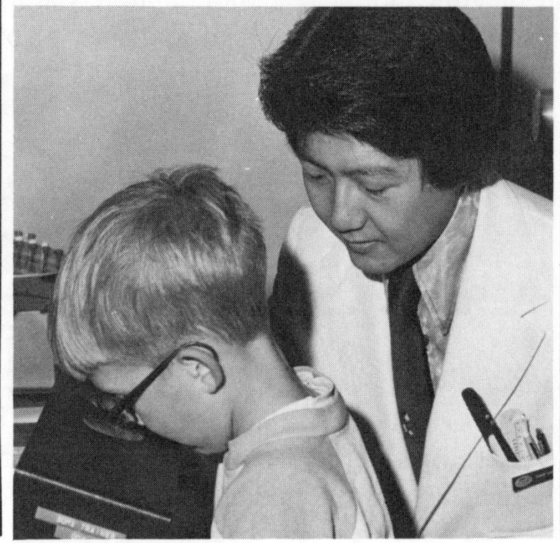

A good decision maker needs the ability to look ahead to see what will happen if certain choices are made. Try to foresee what might happen if you did each of the following; write your prediction next to each action.

What would be the result if you...	Likely results in five years
Got married next year	
Joined the Coast Guard	
Went away to college	
Got a job in a factory	
Travelled abroad for a year	

List here some other possible actions you could take. Predict their results. At left, write whether the action is very, moderately, or slightly important.

Importance	*Possible action*	*Likely result in five years*

8. Overcome Your Barriers

Risk: the possibility of suffering harm or loss; danger.

One of the most common barriers to good decision making is fear of risk. Every choice involves risk. The repercussions can be good or they can cause pain. Even a typical school day has some risks. Consider what these students have to decide:

Mary:	Whether to wear a raincoat or a jacket today.
Doug:	Whether to show up at class without the homework or to cut class.
Maria:	Whether to sign up for track or look for an after-school job.

What are some risks each of these students face?

Mary:____

Doug:____

Maria:____

What happens if the students decide not to take any risks at tall?____________

____

TAKE A RISK TODAY

Risk-taking begins with the small. What is a decision that you have made and acted on today?

____

What happened to you because of that decision and action?

Bad things that happened (losses)______________________________

____

Good things that happened (gains)______________________________

____

The more you learn to move right along, do what you really want to do, and take the risks that go with it, the more confident and active you will become. You will find that once you are an experienced risk-taker you cannot go back. You cannot unlearn your habit of risk taking. You cannot unlearn your confidence. Risk-taking causes failure but also success. With success comes confidence, responsibility, power, and rewards.

THE "I CAN'TS"

Besides fear of risk, another barrier to good decision making is the "I can'ts." Your "I can'ts" are internal messages you give yourself regarding your aptitudes, personality, personal attitudes or prejudices. People frequently express their "I can'ts" by explaining, "I'm just that way!"

What are some of your "I can'ts?"

I can't______________________________________

I can't______________________________________

I can't______________________________________

I can't______________________________________

I can't______________________________________

Are any of your "I can'ts" preventing you from pursuing a desirable goal? What are some of your "I can'ts" that you would like to change? Go ahead and write them down as "I cans!"

I can (and I will)____

I can (and I will)____

I can (and I will)____

THE "YOU CAN'TS" (OTHER PEOPLE'S EXPECTATIONS)

A young man announces that he would rather go to vocational school than college; a girl announces her intention to become a carpenter. Both deviate from what people expect of them.

His parents say, "You can't do that! All your brothers went to college. You should too."

Her parents say, "You don't want a man's job! Why don't you go into nursing or interior decorating?"

Comments like these can be powerful barriers to achieving goals.

What are some of your "you can'ts?"
Some "You can'ts" involve race or sex discrimination, financial need, educational opportunities, the job market, attitudes of society, family responsibilities, and educational background.

List here three possible goals you could decide on. Then evaluate how your parents and best friend would feel about each goal.

________________________ ________________________parent

________________________friend

________________________ ________________________parent

________________________friend

________________________ ________________________parent

________________________friend

9. Summarize Your Information

Once information has been assembled and analyzed, it is time for action. Everyone has fears and worries which form barriers to action. To live in fear is to become immobilized, incapable of action.

The activities in this book all imply possible action. Think of two possible career actions you could now take. Then think of all the fears and worries you have about why these two actions would make you unhappy. List these reasons under Barriers to Action. Then try to think of actions—concrete moves you can make to relieve your fears and worries.

(Sample)
Attractive Career Action: Take course in airline ticketing

Barriers to Action	**Breaking the Barriers to Action**
1. Long inconvenient drive	1. Get in a car pool
2. Ties up 2 nights a week	2. Give self a treat every Friday

BREAKTHROUGH PLANS

Attractive Career Action:__________

Barriers to Action	Breaking the Barriers to Action
1.__________	1.__________
2.__________	2.__________

Attractive Career Action:__________

Barriers to Action	Breaking the Barriers to Action
1.__________	1.__________
2.__________	2.__________

DECISION WRAP-UP

What have you decided while working with this book? Try to form some long-range and immediate goals using a "so that" phrase:

In five years, I will have__________

so that__________

In one year, I will have__________

so that__________

In six months, I will have__________

so that__________

Next week, I will have__________

so that__________

Today, I will have__________

so that__________

PART III: MARKETING YOURSELF

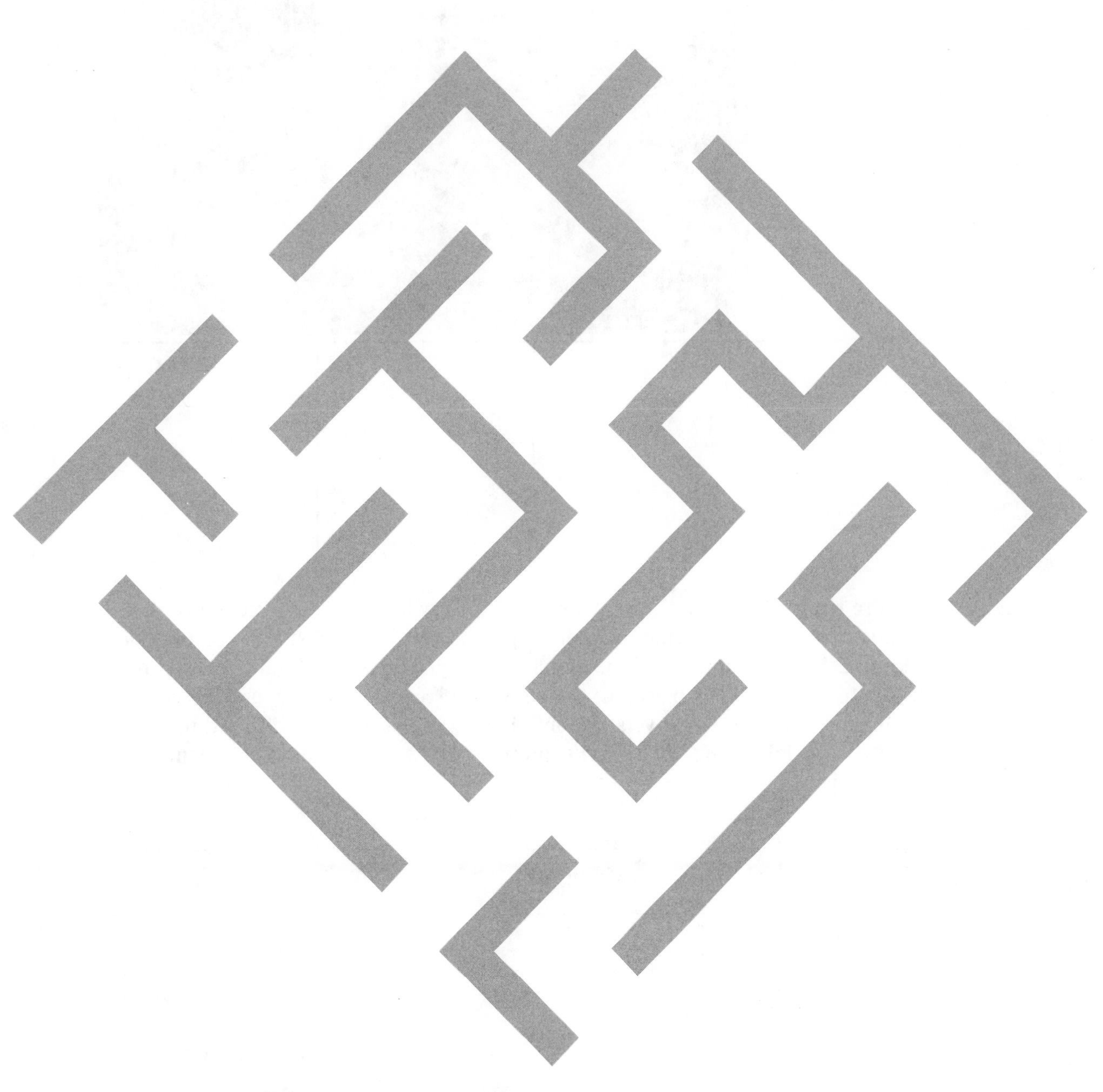

1. A Consumer's Guide to Job Search Strategies

You're ready to play the employment game. It will help you to recognize that it is a game of numbers. A large number of people will vie against you for the good positions. Other big numbers of the employment game are: the hours you will need to devote to a successful job search; the number of résumés, letters, and phone calls you will need to aim at employers; the number of interviews you will need to have a choice between job offers. *Life Plan's* quotient for winning the employment game looks like this:

If you want:	Multiply by	And plan on:
2 job offers	5	10 interviews
10 interviews	5	50 letters, résumés, and phone calls
50 contacts	3	150 hours spent on your job search.

The trickiest part of the employment game is finding leads that will result in job offers. The three best methods are

- applying directly to employers
- asking friends for job leads
- consulting newspaper want ads

The U.S. Department of Labor surveyed ten million job seekers about how they set up interviews that resulted in job offers. The most effective method for every occupation (except clerics) was applying directly to the employer. Answering newspaper ads came in second. Private employment agencies, unions, and tips from friends also helped people win the employment game. Seventy-five percent of the job hunters using many of these methods remained unemployed, so the key to a successful job search will be to combine a variety of job search methods.

NETWORKING

Networking means using your contacts to win the employment game.

Case Study:

Liz has just graduated from college and wants to start a career in public relations. Her parents, family, and college friends have no connections and offer no help. But one of Liz's sorority sisters, Marie Sims, has a father who owns his own public relations agency. Liz asks Marie to see if her father will talk with her.

Mr. Sims agrees to talk with Liz, making it clear that he has no job to offer her. He tells Liz the name of the one agency in town willing to hire inexperienced people. Liz contacts the agency and with some good interviewing techniques, lands her job.

Job Analysis:

Without using her contacts, Liz might never have found her job. Unconsciously, she stumbled on to one of the best resources for finding a job: networking.

Over 90 percent of all jobs are never advertised formally. They are filled through word-of-mouth. People hear that a position is open and apply directly to the employer. Agencies and newspaper ads are never used to fill the vacancy. Studies show that people who get jobs in this manner stay the longest and get the highest raises.

The chart on the next page will help you to apply the principles of networking. It provides space to write down the names of ten people you know who can be of help to you in locating job possibilities. If each of these people can tell you often people who are good potential contacts, you will have a list of 100 possible contacts.

PRELIMINARY LIST OF CONTACTS FOR NETWORKING

MY FRIENDS, RELATIVES AND ACQUAINTANCES	THEIR FRIENDS, RELATIVES AND ACQUAINTANCES WHO MAY BE HELPFUL CONTACTS
1. ______________________	______________________________
	______________________________
2. ______________________	______________________________
	______________________________
3. ______________________	______________________________
	______________________________
4. ______________________	______________________________
	______________________________
5. ______________________	______________________________
	______________________________
6. ______________________	______________________________
	______________________________
7. ______________________	______________________________
	______________________________
8. ______________________	______________________________
	______________________________
9. ______________________	______________________________
	______________________________
10. ______________________	______________________________
	______________________________

Developing Your List for Networking

Name:____

Address:______________________________________

Phone:_______________________________________

How could this person assist you?__________________________

____

How should you approach her/him?__________________________

____

\- -

Name:____

Address:______________________________________

Phone:_______________________________________

How could this person assist you?__________________________

____

How should you approach her/him?__________________________

____

\- -

Name:____

Address:______________________________________

Phone:_______________________________________

How could this person assist you?__________________________

____

How should you approach her/him?__________________________

____

____

NEWSPAPER ADS

Case Study

Tony beats the neighborhood dogs in retrieving his *Sunday Chicago Tribune* off the drive within seconds of its delivery. Moments later, he is engrossed in the *Mid-America Job Guide,* which along with the Help Wanted ads in New York and Los Angeles papers, is one of the thickest lists of jobs available. The paper lists thousands of job openings in alphabetical order. Surely Tony ought to land one of them. Tony looks over the paper and finds one which sounds intriguing: The ad asks that résumés be sent to a post office box.

Tony sends his résumé to the P.O. Box and receives a call from a local employment agency. The job Tony was interested in didn't exist at all; the ad was placed to get clients for the agency.

Tony tries again the following Sunday. One ad gives a telephone number. Tony phones the company. A crisp, professional voice fires dozens of questions. Tony feels he is responding fine, but when he is asked, "Do you own your own car?" Tony says no. The employer replies that this job requires a personal automobile and hangs up. Tony has been screened out before even having an interview.

Another ad asks for a résumé, which Tony promptly mails out. Tony's letter arrives with a batch of 300 other responses to the ad and is given a 15-second reading. A few weeks later he receives a form letter that his was only one of many fine applications received and that his résumé will be kept on file.

Job Analysis

Tony has dead-ended on three job leads. He might have fared better if he had been familiar with *Life Plan's* strategy for successfully using Help Wanted ads.

Timing Your Response

If an advertisement appears in a large Sunday paper such as the *New York Times* or *Chicago Tribune,* send a letter the end of the week following the ad. Mail received earlier in the week is more likely to get lost in the shuffle. There may be 300 responses to an ad where the address of the employer is given and the returns will probably come in like this:

SUNDAY—(day the ad appears)
MONDAY—5 résumés received
TUESDAY—55 résumés received
WEDNESDAY—105 résumés received
THURSDAY—60 résumés received
FRIDAY—20 résumés received
LATER—55 résumés received

People don't usually buy the first pair of shoes they try on, nor do they usually hire the first person they interview. You might even answer ads which appeared a month or two earlier. The position might not yet be filled, or the person hired for the job might not have worked out.

Selecting Ads to Answer

Employers rarely find people who meet all the criteria asked for in the advertisement. If you feel you could handle a job, answer the ad even if you don't have the education or industry experience required.

Answering Blind Ads

About 75 percent of all help wanted ads are *blind ads.* This means that the employer is not identified. Usually the ad asks you to write to a box number. Employers place blind ads to avoid responding to all applicants, to maintain secrecy with other employees or competitors, or to receive more responses than they would if their identity were known. Employment agencies run such ads to gain clients.

You may have an advantage if you can identify the employer placing the ad and apply directly without referring to the ad. One way to "crack" the identity of the ad is to apply directly to all companies who fit the company's description. For example, if the ad states that the company is an electronics firm in southern Texas, send a letter and résumé to all electronics firms in the area.

Responding to Ads by Telephone

Avoid answering any questions over the telephone. Interviewers cannot meet with everyone, so they try to do some preliminary weeding of job candidates over the telephone. If the ad gives a phone number, use it only to set up an appointment. Say something like "I'm at work and can't talk now. Could I come in for an interview?" Once the employer sees your potential, he or she may overlook a job requirement or consider you for another job opening.

Salary Information

Do not give any salary information, even when asked to do so. Even if you appear to be exactly the right person for the job, a too-high or too-low salary figure might disqualify you.

Answering the following questions should help you clarify what an ad is saying and whether you want the job.

Job Advertised:____

Employer:____

Publication:______________________ Date:__________________

1. What requirements and personal qualities should the applicant have?

2. Does the job require "experience"? Have you had nonpaid or educational work which could substitute for job experience?

3. Is any information missing? (Location, salary, duties, or employer's name)

If you cannot answer all these questions from the ad, call the company or use the library to get further information.

4. What are the employer's products or services?

5. Is the name of the person who will do the interviewing mentioned? Is this name real? (Some names are codes to help the company know where you learned about the job.) What is the interviewer's name?

6. What would be your duties in this position?

7. What are the current needs of the company?

8. What is the salary range for this job?

EMPLOYMENT AGENCIES

State Agencies

The government has its own employment agencies. They keep listings of available job openings and try to provide applicants with job leads. State agencies are most frequently used by people who are seeking their first job. Clerical workers often find jobs through state agencies, but people in management tend to avoid them. Studies show that about 60 percent of the people who use state agencies find employment through them.

Private Agencies

There are over 8000 private agencies in the United States. Many specialize in finding people for financial, data processing, health care, office, or communications jobs. Private agencies place only 4 percent of those entering the job market and 15 percent of Americans changing jobs. Some charge the applicant a fee for their services; sometimes the company pays the fee.

Pointers

1. Ask employers you would like to work for which agencies they use. Find out the names of the most competent people at those agencies. Then call that agency and counselor and tell them you were recommended by the firm from which you got their name.

2. Try to find agencies that specialize in your career area, clerical, mechanical, sales, etc. Look for their ads in industry magazines, and the yellow pages of your local phone directory.

3. Fees can be paid by the employer, the applicant (you), or a combination of both. Some fees are negotiated at the time the hiring decision is made. Some fees are high, though; so be sure to find out.

4. Agencies require applicants to sign contracts. Be sure to read any form before signing it. Beware of clauses which require you to pay a fee if you should leave a job within 30 days.

5. You can work with three or four agencies in different parts of the country at the same time. Do not sign up with two agencies which would perform the same services for you, in the same area.

6. Follow the advice the counselors give you regarding your résumé, your appearance, etc. Check with your counselor every few days to see what is being done.

COLLEGE PLACEMENT OFFICES

Most college placement offices offer some of the following services:

- interest and aptitude vocational testing
- current job openings
- reference books, professional journals, business directories and employer information (annual reports, product information, job descriptions)
- career development courses, workshops, job fairs.

Even if you never attended the school near your home, try to take advantage of their services.

Rank the three job search methods that would be best for you, by numbering them 1, 2, and 3 below.

______ Apply directly to employer

______ Ask friends or relatives

______ Answer newspaper ads

______ Private employment agencies

______ State employment services

______ School placement offices

______ Place newspaper ads

______ Answer ads in professional or trade journals

2. Résumés, Applications, and Cover Letters

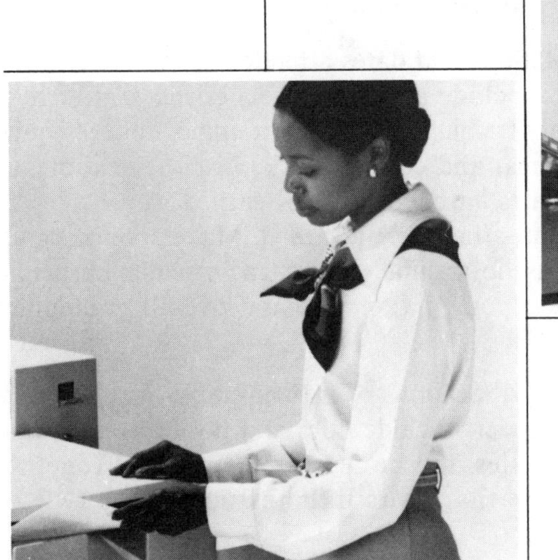

A STEP-BY-STEP GUIDE FOR RÉSUMÉ PREPARATION

Your résumé (pronounced rez-u-may) is your advertisement for yourself. The résumé is the basic door-opener for careers other than entry-level, clerical positions and some blue-collar jobs where an application form may be sufficient information. The résumé accompanies letters of application to employers and is left with them after interviews as a reminder of your qualifications. It introduces you to an employer and advertises your most important assets. Your résumé should "package" your qualifications in an appealing wrapper that an employer will not pass up.

What Should Be in a Résumé:

- Identification section—Who you are.
- Job objective section—What you want to do.
- Background section—What you have to offer in the way of education, experience, and personal experience.

Résumés may take two different formats: chronological and functional.

CHRONOLOGICAL RÉSUMÉ FORMAT

Name Address Phone number (Include area code)	Personal information. (Some experts advise specifying marital status, height, weight and health, but the majority feel the disadvantages outweigh the advantages and suggest omitting personal information.)
JOB OBJECTIVE	A brief statement indicating position sought and type of organization preferred. (Include only if the same objective can be used for all applications.)
EDUCATION	Name institutions and dates attended in reverse chronological order. Include all learning experiences after high school: military training, on-the job training, college equivalency programs, and college work. List the schools attended, the dates enrolled, degrees earned, certificates or licenses and dates they were awarded. Make note of significant honors, scholarships, and extracurricular participation. Put down your major field and overall gradepoint average.
WORK EXPERIENCE	List names and locations of former employers in reverse chronological order. Include titles and positions held, major responsibilities and duties. Omit or group together work experience that bears little relationship to type of work you seek.
MILITARY OBLIGATION	If applicable, summarize military experience and show draft classification.
MISCELLANEOUS INFORMATION	Describe any relevant points not covered elsewhere in résumé: school honors, organization memberships, travel experience, foreign language expertise, outside interests.
REFERENCES	References will be furnished upon request. Do not list references on the résumé. This will enable you to have a flexible list of references that can be changed as needed.

RULES FOR RÉSUMÉ WRITING

1. Write short, concise sentences. Use as few words as necessary to express your accomplishments.
2. Use action verbs to begin each sentence or phrase. Examples: created, exhibited, mobilized, repaired, designed, motivated, presented.
3. Use the vocabulary or "jargon" of your field, but avoid becoming overly technical. Speak a language the person reading the résumé will understand.

4. List specific accomplishments and results. Use numbers when possible.
   - Increased production by 25 percent.
   - Devised sales campaign that netted $1500 for class treasury.
   - Won *Atlantic Monthly* national short story writing contest.
5. Convey one selling point at a time. Don't confuse your accomplishments by grouping too many ideas together.
6. Put the concerns of your potential employer ahead of your own needs. This may mean rewriting your résumé several times in order to focus on various aspects of your accomplishments.
7. Don't get too personal. No one usually cares that you do needlework or collect trains. Do not include your picture on the résumé.
8. Type the résumé in a clear, clean typeface. Commercial typing services can do the final typing. The layout should look professional and entice people to read it. Retain sufficient white space, leaving at least one-inch margins, and double space between paragraphs.
9. Fit your résumé on one page of 8½ x 11 inch paper. Employers receive many résumés each week and often spend as little as 15 seconds on each one.
10. Have someone proofread your final copy for any spelling errors.
11. Have the résumé professionally printed (photo-offset is best). Select off-white, beige, or light gray paper, a heavy grade quality. Buy from the printer matching envelopes and blank pieces of paper for writing cover letters.

RÉSUMÉ STRATEGY NO. 1: TAKING INVENTORY

When looking for a job you become your own advertising manager. Your task is to sell yourself. Any good sales campaign begins with an inventory of selling points.

List all learning experiences, including military training, on-the job training, and college equivalency programs which you have participated in. If you went to college, list the dates enrolled, any degrees earned, and the dates they were awarded. List any full-time work experience here, beginning with your current job and listing the jobs backwards.

RÉSUMÉ STRATEGY NO. 2: ACCOMPLISHMENT INVENTORY

The following exercise lists action verbs. Use them to create phrases that explain your accomplishments. Try to think of things you have done in which you have performed one of the actions listed.

Handled____

Taught____

Developed____

Created____

Expanded____

Presented____

Organized____

Operated____

Designed____

Improved____

Conducted____

Administered____

Established____

Analyzed____

Invented____

Evaluated____

Exhibited____

Supported____

Reorganized____

Sold____

Presented____

Delivered____

RÉSUMÉ STRATEGY NO. 3: COMPOSING YOUR CAREER OBJECTIVE

To formulate a career objective, begin by defining your strongest skill areas. List four accomplishments, things you are proud of. Begin the list with a series of action words. Here is a list of action words that could be used to begin each sentence:

edited	generated	surveyed	developed	supervised
lead	earned	planned	handled	read
organized	won	conducted	revised	persuaded
presided	sold	wrote	coordinated	taught

Accomplishments	Talent or Skills
(sample) Edited school yearbook	good writer; leadership
1.	
2.	
3.	
4.	

Now ask yourself, "What qualities or abilities do I have that enabled me to do this? In the column to the right summarize the skills or inborn abilities that enabled you to make each of these accomplishments.

Name two positions you would like to seek:

____

Now name two skills which you believe you have and which would be needed in these careers:

____

Now try to compose a job objective. It can be phrased something like this:

I would like to use my____________________ and____________________

skills in a____

or____ position.

RÉSUMÉ STRATEGY NO. 4: COMPOSING THE FIRST DRAFT

Name:
Address:
City & State:
Phone:

Permanent Address:

Phone:

JOB OBJECTIVE: I would like to use my________________ and ________________ skills in a ____________________ or ____________________ position.

EDUCATION:

____

____

____

____

____

MILITARY STATUS:

____

WORK EXPERIENCE:

____

____

____

____

____

____

____

References available upon request.

RÉSUMÉ STRATEGY NO. 5: CRITIQUING YOUR RÉSUMÉ

Always have some competent person proofread and evaluate your résumé before duplicating it. Here is an evaluation form to help in making concrete suggestions for improvement.

RÉSUMÉ CHECKLIST	SUGGESTIONS FOR IMPROVEMENT
Does the overall appearance make you want to read the résumé?	
Are there any typos or misspellings?	
Are the margins clear and consistent?	
Could the layout be improved?	
Is the résumé well typed on one page?	
Is there any irrelevant information?	
Could the résumé be shortened?	
Are all periods of time accounted for?	
Does the résumé begin with the most recent accomplishment?	
Is the writing style clear, concise, and understandable?	
Do action verbs begin each sentence or phrase?	
Does the résumé stress accomplishments and results?	
Is all important information included?	

RÉSUMÉ

Henry Furner
927 Myra Street #8A
San Francisco, CA 90430
(903) 875-8736

JOB OBJECTIVE: I would like any kind of position relating to restaurant operation in the California area.

EDUCATION:
Freeport Boy's Prep—graduated 1975—college prep track.
University of Southern Illinois—Carbondale IL—Bachelors in restaurant management. Finished in top half of class.

EXPERIENCE:
19__-__ Worked and travelled in Europe.
19__-__ Financial Credit Coordinator
Household Credit Corp. Winnetka IL
19__-__ Associate Manager
JoJo's Restaurants Buffalo Grove IL
19__-__ Credit & Collection officer and customer service agent
General Tire Company Elk Grove IL

CAREER ACCOMPLISHMENTS:
Upgraded customer service standards within a large retail tire company.
Assisted in the design and implementation of a new code of restaurant table service standards.
Established a high volume of ''repeat'' business for a large consumer finance institution.
Head waiter of a Swiss summer resort and assistant to the manager.

HOBBIES: Jogging, skiing, photography

Miscellaneous: Fluent in French and Italian
Member of Phi Alpha Theta International Honor Society in History

RÉSUMÉ STRATEGY NO. 6: SELECTING REFERENCES

Employers check with references to verify statements made on your application regarding salary, length of employment and the reason for leaving the company. They also want to obtain your previous employers' estimates of your work habits and strong and weak points.

It is best to have two sets of references. Use those you think would most impress an employer for jobs you really want. Use the second list for jobs you will only accept in desperation.

List previous employers, teachers who know your skills for at least two references. Pastors or people in the community who can vouch for your personal character may be used for a third.

Always get the permission of the person you list as a reference. References are typed on a separate sheet of paper and given to an employer when requested.

Question

Micky applied for a position at a large company and was informed that the company will run a character check on her. Having nothing to hide, she gave her permission. She was not offered the job, so she suspects that whoever did the checking discovered something negative about her. Does she have the right to know who said something about her and whether the information was correct?

Answer

Under the Fair Credit Reporting Act, Micky is entitled to find out who did the investigating and what was reported. If the information is false, she has the right to have it corrected. The reporting agency must let the employer know that a mistake was made.

Your References

Name____

Position____________________ Company____________________

Address____________________________ Phone____________

Name____

Position____________________ Company____________________

Address____________________________ Phone____________

CORRESPONDENCE THAT WINS INTERVIEWS

Never mail your résumé to any employer without writing a personalized cover letter. Here is a sample newspaper ad and responding cover letter.

> We are a growing, aggressive consumer goods company looking for an experienced Accounting Supervisor to assist in our accounting department. Duties will include supervision of clerks in the areas of inventory, accounts payable and accts. receivable.
>
> We offer good starting salary, insurance benefits and company-paid profit sharing.
>
> Write Irene Kimball, Sr. Accountant,
> The Stroup Exchange, Inc.
> 3399 Dundee Rd. N. E.
> Perkins, Iowa 52301

Notice that the ad asks for an experienced worker and that the duties will include supervision of others. Check to see what kinds of work will be handled by the department. Experience in these areas should be mentioned in the cover letter.

At the same time, you should be careful not to overload the letter with details—remember that you will want to have something to say during the interview as well. The résumé and the cover letter should give the "big picture" accurately, but should not be so long that the reader loses interest.

Use stationery which matches the size and color of your résumé. Off-white, beige, or gray papers are best.

Donna Burke
809 Crandall Drive
Cedar Rapids IA 52402
318-242-8995

Write to a person who has the power to hire you, using name and title. Always direct your letter to a particular person. Call the company and request a name if none is given in the ad.

Ms. Irene Kimball
Senior Accountant
The Stroup Exchange, Inc.
3399 Dundee Rd. N.E.
Perkins, Iowa, 52301

Dear Ms. Kimball:

Identify the job for which you are applying.

Please consider me for the position advertised in the September 4, 198__ *Chicago Tribune.*

The enclosed résumé highlights my educational qualifications to supervise employees and prepare budget reports.

Enumerate the qualifications you have which the employer requires.

My experience supervising 15 waitresses at Keystone, Colorado has sharpened my ability to motivate, oversee, and discipline employees in any setting. I have had 30 hours college work in accounting and am familiar with most reporting methods.

State that you will take the initiative in contacting the employer.

Please expect my call next week. I hope we can meet for an interview.

Thank you.

Sincerely,

Type your letter professionally, limiting it to one page.

Donna Burke

Sign your full name. Use a blue felt tip pen. These pens give a forcefulness that may help.

Here are other guidelines for writing effective letters: Keep your letters short and simple. Avoid flowery words; be direct. Keep paragraphs short—no more than 5 or 6 lines each. Double spacing between paragraphs adds to readability.

APPLICATION FORMS

Complete any application form as neatly as possible. If it is sloppy, it suggests that you are impatient or inattentive to detail. If it is extremely neat and complete, it suggests that you are methodical, patient, and detail-oriented.

Use only black or blue pen. Your pen should let you print neatly without blobs, smudges, or smears. A fine-point makes it easier to print small. Avoid erasures and cross-outs; they indicate concern or anxiety about that topic.

Read the instructions before writing any date on an application. Many applications begin with general instructions, such as "Print in ink" or "Type." Since employers want to hire people who can follow instructions on the job, the way you follow directions on the application gives an indication of what kind of employee you would be.

If an application question does not apply to you, make a short dash (–). If an honest answer to a question might screen you out of the candidates job, leave it blank or write "will explain on interview." Never admit anything negative about yourself without the opportunity to give an explanation.

Name

List your name just as it is asked for on an application. Application forms usually ask for last name first, then first name, then middle name or initial. Do not use nicknames unless there is a special blank for it. You want to show that you are businesslike, so use your complete legal name. Most applications require a signature at the end. Sign your name as you sign checks or legal papers.

Address

All applications ask for your current address. Some ask for previous addresses or your permanent address. Be prepared with house numbers and zip codes.

Date of Birth

Date of birth and age can only be asked before hiring to satisfy minimum age requirements. Answer this question if you are a minor or might appear under age. Put a dash if you are obviously a mature adult.

Telephone Number

Since many employers contact applicants by phone rather than by mail, it is extremely important that you list a phone number that is likely to be answered during the day. If no one can answer your phone, list the number of someone reliable who can accept your messages.

Print the number, including area code, completely and neatly. If the number is an office with an extension, include the extension number. It is a good idea to list two numbers so if the first number is unanswered, people can try the second.

Social Security Number

Be sure you have your correct number with you and list it legibly. If you do not have a social security number, apply for one at your nearest social security office or post office.

Position Sought

You should know what you want to do. If you respond, "any job," you won't make a strong impression. List the title of the job you want and then put in parentheses "or similar position." This shows an employer that you have a specific goal but are open to other possibilities. If you have had a job, it is best if the job applied for represents a step forward.

Salary Expected

The best response to salary queries on applications is "Open." You then don't commit yourself to a figure that is too high or too low. When interviewing for a job, you should know the market value of the position. Salaries are computed by hour, week, two-week period, month, or year. You should compute your desired salary in terms of each pay period.

Education

Most applications ask detailed questions about your education, so be prepared with schools you attended and the dates you were enrolled. If there is not enough space, list only schools from which you graduated.

When asked about further schooling, answer with courses that would benefit you in the career you want. If you plan future schooling that is not related to your career path, the employer may conclude that you are not committed to your career. Leave future schooling blank if you are not sure of your goals. If asked how your education was financed, list the percentage of tuition and expenses which you earned. For example, "Earned 25 percent of college tuition and expenses."

Activities

Many applications provide a special, separate section for volunteer activities. Volunteer work can develop important skills and responsibility. If there is no special section for volunteer work, list it under Work Experience.

Previous Employment

Employers find this section extremely important. Be prepared with names and addresses of former employers. List your present job first and move back in time. If you have no work experience, leave this section blank. Between the education section and the work experience section, all years should be explained. Under "reason for leaving," make positive statements about yourself and your goals rather than being negative about your former employers. In other words, say "desired more responsibility" rather than "boss was very hard to get along with."

Remember when answering questions about future plans that employers want to hire people who will stay with the company. Answer such questions with a response, "as long as my skills are being fully tapped" if that can honestly be said.

Be sure that all times are accounted for, as gaps in an application can indicate that you are trying to cover up something negative.

Military Status

Most applications ask about military background. If you were honorably discharged, list all the data. If you received less than an honorable discharge, leave the section blank. Be prepared to discuss your military experience in the interview. Put a dash if you were never in the service, registered for the draft, or in reserves.

References

A reference is a person who will testify to your character and abilities as an employee. Employers often contact references, so list them carefully; always ask permission before listing anyone as a reference. People commonly used for references include former employers, supervisors and co-workers, former teachers, friends who have jobs indicating responsibility, and people who have known you in a volunteer capacity. Family members should not be listed.

Be prepared with names, addresses, and phone numbers of three people who have agreed to provide a reference.

3. The Interview

The interview is the single most important step in winning the employment game. The interview is your chance to determine if you would like to work for an employer and the employer's chance to determine your suitability for a job. Too many interviews are psychological games, parent-child confrontations where the interviewer (the parent) asks questions of the prospective employee (the child). Think of the interview as a negotiation where the basic issues are: What do I want? What do you want? How can we both get what we want?

INTERVIEW STRATEGY NO. 1: WINNING INTERVIEWS

After an employer has received your résumé, you should telephone to schedule an interview. Your call should have a definite opening, middle, and conclusion.

Have a pen or pencil and paper ready. Telephone from a quiet place. Try not to use a pay telephone. Ask for the person it is best to speak with—the person who has the power to hire you.

State who you are, that you sent a letter and résumé, and why you are qualified for the job you seek. Set up a meeting at which your employment could be discussed. Write down the details of the interview: name of interviewer; date and time; address and room number; travelling directions, if needed.

Overheard on the Party Line: "Tactics for Dealing With Secretaries"

Ask directly for the person you want.	"This is Edward Arnold. May I speak with Mr. Barrett?"
	"What is this in reference to?"
State your purpose.	"I would like to discuss the landscaping position you have open."
	"Perhaps I can help you."
If you can't get through, try to get an appointment.	"Yes, could I arrange a meeting with Mr. Barrett to discuss this position early next week?"
	"Mr. Barrett's schedule is filled for next week".
Try again to get an appointment.	"Then, when would be a good time for me to call back to speak with him? He has received my résumé and I'm anxious to discuss the opening with him."
	"Mr. Barrett will contact you if he is interested in your résumé."

Try to avoid the secretary if he or she is a zealous gatekeeper. Call back before 8:30, at lunchtime, or after 5:00. Many bosses work long days, while their secretaries leave on time.

Keep a record of your telephone contacts. Write down the name of the company, the person(s) with whom you talk, and the results. A sample record form is supplied on the next page.

Telephone Contact Form

Company's name____

Contact person____

Job you seek____

Your special qualifications to hold that job____

____

Results of telephone call____

____

_ _

Company's name____

Contact person____

Job you seek____

Your special qualifications to hold that job____

____

Results of telephone call____

____

_ _

Company's name____

Contact person____

Job you seek____

Your special qualifications to hold that job____

____

Results of telephone call____

____

YOUR LEGAL RIGHTS

Knowing your rights means knowing the law.

It is the law that when applying for a job you cannot be discriminated against because of race, color, religion, sex, age, or in many cases, certain physical or mental handicaps.

Employers interpret anti-bias laws differently and may ask questions which could be discriminatory. Knowing what can be asked legitimately in interviews and applications can protect your rights.

INTERVIEW STRATEGY NO. 2: KNOW YOUR RIGHTS

To be comfortable in an interview it is helpful to understand the rights and responsibilities of both the applicant and the employer.

Rights and Responsibilities of Employer

- To establish lines of communication, make you feel comfortable.
- To evaluate your appearance and personal demeanor.
- To evaluate the relevancy of your education to the job.
- To understand your work experience.
- To explain the responsibilities of the job opening.
- To explain company benefits, vacation policies.
- To notify you when a decision will be made on the opening.
- To determine your interest in the job.
- To administer any tests relating to the job.
- To assess your suitability for the job.
- To negotiate acceptable salary.

Rights and Responsibilities of Applicant

- To highlight aspects of your education that best reveal your abilities and background.
- To communicate the achievements of your past life, whether it be work or volunteer activity.
- To communicate a sincere interest by asking knowledgable questions about the position.
- To discover what future or career path may result if you accept this position.
- To negotiate an acceptable salary.
- To reach an understanding of the duties and rewards associated with the position.
- To persuade the employer to hire you.
- To determine the employer's interest in you.
- To establish basis for continuing communication.

WHAT QUESTIONS CAN AN EMPLOYER LEGALLY ASK?

	Acceptable Inquiry	Illegitimate Inquiry
Name	What names or nicknames have you used in your past work?	What is your maiden name? What is your original name?
Address and Phone	What is your address Phone number? How long have you resided in the city and state where the employer is located? If you have no phone, where can we reach you?	Do you rent or own your own home? What is your birthplace? What is the birthplace of your parents, spouse, or relatives?
Creed or Religion		What is your religion? What church do you attend? What religious holidays do you observe?
Appearance	What general distinguishing physical characteristics (such as scars) do you have? Height may be requested only when it is a bona fide occupational requirement.	What is the color of your hair, eyes, skin? What is your weight? (Photographs may be required *after* hiring.)
Age	Can you furnish proof of age if you are hired? Date of birth may be needed to: (1) maintain apprenticeship requirements (2) satisfy state or federal minimum age statutes (3) administer retirement, pension, or employee benefits	What is the date of your birth? What is your age?
Education	What schools did you attend? What degrees were earned? What academic work is in progress? What vocational training have you had on your own or through an employer?	

	Acceptable Inquiry	Illegitimate Inquiry
Citizenship	Are you a U.S. citizen? Do you have the legal right to work in the U.S.?	Are you a naturalized or native-born citizen? Do you intend to become a citizen? Of what country are you a citizen?
National Origin		What is your ancestry? What is the nationality of your parents or spouse? (Unless the employee is an organization promoting a particular national heritage.)
Language	What languages do you speak or write fluently?	What is your native tongue? What language is spoken in your home? How did you acquire fluency in another language?
Relatives and Dependents	What relatives are already employed by this company? Name and address of person to be notified in case of emergency.	Do you have any children? If so, how old are they? Who lives in your household? What childcare provisions do you have?
Sex and Marital Status		Do you want to be addressed as Mrs. Miss or Ms.? What is your sex? Are you married? Divorced? Widowed? Single?
Military Experience	Are you a veteran? Did the military provide you with job training? Have you been notified to report for duty in the armed forces?	What foreign military experience have you had? Some states forbid questions such as: are you eligible for military service? what were the dates and conditions of your discharge?
Organizations	To what union, trade, or professional societies do you belong	What clubs or organizations do you belong to?

	Acceptable Inquiry	Illegitimate Inquiry
References	Names and addresses of persons willing to provide professional or character references? Who suggested that you apply? Do you have any objections if we check your employer for references?	Who is your pastor or religious leader?
Arrest Record	How many times have you been convicted of a felony? What were you convicted for?	Have you ever been arrested?
Health and Handicaps	Do you have any physical or mental impairments that could prevent you from perfoming on this job? Are there any duties you could not perform because of health reasons?	
Financial Status		Have your wages ever been attached or garnisheed?
Employment History	How many years of experience do you have? What are the names and address of previous employers? What were your duties? How long did you hold the job? Why did you leave your previous job? Why do you seek this position?	

ASSERTIVE INTERVIEWING TECHNIQUES

Communicating honestly, directly, and in an appropriate way is vital for winning the employment game. What you say, the tone of your voice, even your posture can communicate your basic self-respect. Unfortunately, interviewers do not always act within the law, and it is necessary to assert your rights to win good employment.

Some people are assertive, some nonassertive, some aggressive. The most successful are assertive. Recognizing the difference between them can make acting assertively easier to master.

Nonassertive behavior

Nonassertive people violate their own rights by failing to express their feelings, thoughts, and beliefs. They often act in an apologetic, self-effacing manner that encourages others to disregard and violate their personal rights. A nonassertive person's behavior says, "I don't count; you can take advantage of me. My feelings don't matter, only yours do. I'm nothing. You're superior."

Assertive behavior

Assertive people believe in their basic human rights. They approach others as human beings, not adversaries. They stand up for their rights, needs, desires, and beliefs. They articulate their thoughts honestly and directly without violating other people's rights. An assertive person communicates, "I'm O.K. and so are you."

Aggressive behavior

Aggressive people stand up for their rights, thoughts, feelings, and beliefs but attack others, violating the rights of other people. They dominate to get their points across. Their message says, "I must win; you're unimportant. This is what I feel; your feelings don't count. This is what I think; you're stupid for believing differently."

CHECK YOUR BODY LANGUAGE

We can communicate as much with what our bodies say as with what we way in our speech. Below are some examples to think over in assessing how assertive body language is. Mark each one either *S* or *I*, after you have thought over the response each action would bring.

S: Satisfactory
I: Improvement needed

Assertive

____Direct eye contact

____Open, relaxed facial expression

____Firm voice

____Emphasize key words

____Well-balanced posture

____Relaxed demeanor

____Gesture to emphasize key points

Aggressive

____Stare into distance

____Bored expression

____Tight-lipped

____Clenched teeth

____Rapid speech

____Overly loud

____Condescending manner

____Pound fists

____Point finger

____Hands on hips

Nonassertive

____Downcast eyes

____Rapid blinking

____Inappropriate smiling

____Inappropriate laughter

____Biting lips

____Wetting lips

____Clearing throat

____Wrinkled forehead

____Very soft speech

____Whine

____Cover mouth when speaking

____Excessive nodding

____Fiddle with glasses, jewelry

INVESTIGATE THE EMPLOYER

The more prepared you are for an interview, the more likely that you will win the employment game. Many employers reject applicants because they show little interest or enthusiasm for the company.

Thoroughly research every company with which you interview. Possible sources for finding out about any organization include:

- leaflets, brochures and annual reports published by the company
- advertisements for its products
- job description for the job you are seeking
- employees of the organization
- trade journals and magazines found in libraries
- the local Chamber of Commerce
- customers who use the company's products
- the local library's files of newspapers and clippings
- business directories to be found in library
- the local Better Business Bureau

If the company that you are interested in has recently built new additions, or has purchased land, and is building new factories or offices, you may be able to find articles in back issues of newspapers in the area, which will tell what the expansion will be. This is a good source of advance information about possible jobs at any time. Even though a company has not advertised for applicants, you can assume that if they are building new additions, that they will need at least some new employees at the new location.

Employer Inventory

List your findings about the job openings you are interested in pursuing.

Company:____

Address:____

Phone:____

Contact Person:____________________________________

Skills that should be emphasized with this employer:____________________

____

Deficiencies in your background that this employer may have reservations about:______

____

How can you overcome this deficiency?____________________________

____

\- -

Company:____

Address:____

Phone:____

Contact Person:____________________________________

Skills that should be emphasized with this employer:____________________

____

Deficiencies in your background that this employer may have reservations about:______

____

How can you overcome this deficiency?____________________________

____

REHEARSING THE INTERVIEW

In order to see yourself as others see you, try role playing an interview as though you were an actor on stage. Role playing will put you at ease with potential interview situations and will prepare you to answer many questions.

Levels of Role Play

1. Role play alone with the aid of a mirror. Sit in front of the mirror. Ask yourself questions and answer them. Speak aloud in a firm, clear voice, answering your own questions. Watch yourself as you speak. Is your voice trembling? Are there any nervous gestures? If you have any nervous gestures try folding your hands in your lap and folding them on a table. Keep working until you sound and appear self-assured, calm, and knowledgable on your background and potential.

2. Tape record an interview. Involve friends as the interviewers and try to get their feedback on how you sound.

3. If available use a videotape recorder and tape yourself in a mock interview. Video equipment is becoming readily available through schools and professional organizations. Get a friend to act as the interviewer and to critique your performance.

Summary: Checklist for Winning the Employment Game

Put a check as you actually fulfill steps to gaining full employment.

_______ You use a variety of job search methods.

_______ Apply directly to employer.

_______ Ask friends or relatives for job leads.

_______ Answer newspaper ads.

_______ Register with private employment agency.

_______ Register with state employment agency.

_______ Check with school placement offices.

_______ Place newspaper ad.

_______ Answer ads in professional or trade journals.

_______ You follow the step-by-step guide for résumé preparation.

_______ You notify people you wish to list as references.

_______ You write a customized cover letter for each résumé that you mail out.

_______ You use follow-up telephone calls to gain interviews.

_______ You role-play the interview.

_______ You research the salary range you can legitimately expect.

_______ You research each company you have an interview with.

_______ You arrive for interviews punctually.

_______ You dress appropriately for the interview.

_______ You remember the name of the interviewer.

_______ You answer all questions assertively and clearly.

Remember that you are changing from time to time and that the job requirements in the world are changing, too. At the same time that you may be experiencing a growing interest in the environment and in ecology, the world may be developing a growing need for people to work in these areas, also.

From time to time, you will want to assess your skills and the needs of the job market. If you have new interests, you will want to develop some new skills to help you move into new areas. Whenever you feel the need to reassess your job potential, or your career goals, you will want to revamp your *Life Plan*.

At times of change in your career goals, you will follow the same steps that you have followed in using this workbook, and in working with your career guidance advisor in school or in another service organization. You may want to use the actual forms that appear in this book, and you may want to add to them the personal techniques that you have developed for yourself.

Life Planning In a Changing World

If you are approaching a time of great changes in other areas of your life, you will want to do a very thorough job of making the most of your job potential in changing careers. For instance, if you want to change jobs at mid-life, you will want to consider that a job may mean different things to you than it did when you were in your twenties. For a person of forty, perhaps the job will have to take the place of a lot of the home life that occupied the person's time when there were children to be cared for.

Later on, there may come a time when you will want to make a job change at the usual age that many people consider retirement. Perhaps that will be just the time that you will want to pursue a hobby that can be turned into a part or full–time job. Perhaps you know someone of sixty-five or so who has always wanted to be a ceramics instructor, and now that the person has reached retirement age it is possible to do just that.

Many life changes will bring with them changes in the needs that you have for a job. An athlete may become disabled and not be able to make a living at sports, but may discover a talent for sales and management. A young couple with small children may find an increasing need for money, in excess of the amounts they originally planned when they chose their careers. Inflation, recessions, military service and other external conditions of life may intervene to cause your plans to change all through your life. Don't let it throw you; use it to your advantage and make the time of change a time of growth for your own good. It can be done.

LIFE CHANGES THAT CAN AFFECT CAREER AND LIFE PLANNING

Listed below are a number of changes which could occur within a normal life span. Any of these changes might cause a need for further examination and changes in life planning. Read through this list, and consider which changes could take place in your own life. Use the lines provided below to write in additional changes which you can imagine possibly occurring in your own life. Try to estimate when such changes might occur, and consider how they would affect your career plans at that time.

Money problems that make more income essential.

Marriage and the birth of children.

The death of a loved one or family member.

Illness in the family that necessitates someone staying at home with the patient.

A move to a new town where the industries or businesses are different.

A technological development that does away with an accustomed job.

An economic downturn that makes an employer shut down the business.

The development of an ulcer or other digestive problem that requires a less stressful work environment.

The industry that has supported the town you live in closes down.

You have always "messed around" with wood sculpture. You discover it will bring in more money than the job you have been working at for several years.

Your parents are elderly and could use some help. They live in an industrial city where most jobs are in the steel industry.

____

____

____

____

____

Bibliography of Related Reading

BIBLIOGRAPHY OF RELATED READING

What Color Is Your Parachute? Richard Nelson Bolles, Ten Speed Press, Berkley, 1983.

You're Fired, B. A. Dickman, Gracelaine Publications, Montgomery, Alabama, 1978.

Job Hunting Secrets and Tactics, Kirby W. Stanat and Patrick Reardon, New Century/Westwind, Milwaukee, 1977.

How To Land A Better Job, Catherine S. Lott and Oscar C. Lott, National Textbook Company, Linconwood, Illinois, 1984.

Getting A Job In Today's Competitive Market, Adele Lewis and William Lewis, Barron's Educational Series, Woodbury, New York, 1982.

Jobs Of The Future, Marvin J. Cetron with Marcia Appel, McGraw-Hill Book Company, New York, 1984.

Where The Jobs Are, William J. McBurney, Jr., Chilton Book Company, Radnor, Pennsylvania, 1982.

VGM CAREER HORIZONS SERIES

CAREER PLANNING

How to Land a Better Job
How to Write a Winning Résumé
Life Plan
Planning Your College Education
Planning your Military Career

SURVIVAL GUIDES

High School Survival Guide
College Survival Guide

OPPORTUNITIES IN

Available in both paperback and hardbound editions

Accounting Careers
Acting Careers
Advertising Careers
Airline Careers
Animal and Pet Care
Appraising Valuation Science
Architecture
Automotive Service
Banking
Beauty Culture
Biological Sciences
Book Publishing
Broadcasting Careers
Building Construction Trades
Cable Television
Carpentry
Chemical Engineering
Chemistry
Chiropractic Health Care
Civil Engineering
Commercial Art and Graphic Design
Computer Science Careers
Counseling & Guidance
Dance
Data Processing Careers
Dental Care
Drafting Careers
Electrical Trades
Electronic and Electrical Engineering
Energy Careers
Engineering Technology
Environmental Careers
Fashion
Federal Government Careers
Film Careers
Financial Careers
Fire Protection Services
Food Services
Foreign Language Careers
Forestry Careers
Free Lance Writing
Government Service
Graphic Communications
Health and Medical Careers
Hospital Administration
Hotel & Motel Management
Industrial Design
Interior Design
Journalism Careers
Landscape Architecture
Law Careers
Law Enforcement and Criminal Justice
Library and Information Science
Machine Shop Trades
Magazine Publishing
Management
Marine & Maritime
Materials Science
Mechanical Engineering
Microelectronics
Modeling Careers
Music Careers
Nursing Careers
Occupational Therapy
Office Occupations
Opticianry
Optometry
Packaging Science
Paralegal Careers
Paramedical Careers
Personnel Management
Pharmacy Careers
Photography
Physical Therapy
Podiatric Medicine
Printing Careers
Psychiatry
Psychology
Public Relations Careers
Real Estate
Recreation and Leisure
Refrigeration and Air Conditioning
Religious Service
Sales & Marketing
Secretarial Careers
Securities Industry
Sports & Athletics
Sports Medicine
State and Local Government
Teaching Careers
Technical Communications
Telecommunications
Theatrical Design & Production
Transportation
Travel Careers
Veterinary Medicine
Word Processing
Writing Careers
Your Own Service Business

WOMEN IN

Available in both paperback and hardbound editions

Communications
Engineering
Finance
Government
Management
Science
Their Own Business

VGM Career Horizons
A Division of National Textbook Company
4255 West Touhy Avenue
Lincolnwood, Illinois 60646-1975 U.S.A.